The Positive Relationships Classroom Activity Book

T0385304

from the author

Games and Activities for Exploring Feelings with Children
Giving Children the Confidence to Navigate Emotions and Friendships
Vanessa Rogers
ISBN 978 1 84905 222 1
eISBN 978 0 85700 459 8

Educating Young People About Pornography
Relationships and Sex Education (RSE) Activities for 11–19 year olds
Vanessa Rogers
ISBN 978 1 78775 833 9
eISBN 978 1 78775 834 6

Let's Talk Relationships
Activities for Exploring Love, Sex, Friendship and Family with Young People
Vanessa Rogers
ISBN 978 1 84905 136 1
eISBN 978 0 85700 340 9

of related interest

The Every Body Book
The LGBTQ+ Inclusive Guide for Kids about Sex, Gender, Bodies, and Families
Rachel E. Simon, LCSW
Illustrated by Noah Grigni
ISBN 978 1 78775 173 6
eISBN 978 1 78775 174 3

Simple Stuff to Get Kids Self-Regulating in School
Awesome and in Control Lesson Plans, Worksheets, and Strategies for Learning
Lauren Brukner & Lauren Liebstein Singer
Illustrated by John Smisson
ISBN 978 1 78592 761 4
eISBN 978 1 78450 623 0

Emotion Coaching with Children and Young People in Schools
Promoting Positive Behavior, Wellbeing and Resilience
Louise Gilbert, Licette Gus and Janet Rose
Foreword by John Gottman, PhD
ISBN 978 1 78775 798 1
eISBN 978 1 78775 799 8

THE POSITIVE RELATIONSHIPS CLASSROOM ACTIVITY BOOK

TEACHING CHILDREN AGE 7-11 ABOUT FRIENDSHIP, FAMILY AND RESPECTFUL RELATIONSHIPS

VANESSA ROGERS

Jessica Kingsley Publishers
London and Philadelphia

First published in Great Britain in 2025 by Jessica Kingsley Publishers
An imprint of John Murray Press

1

A CIP catalogue record for this title is available from the British Library and the Library of Congress

ISBN 978 1 83997 489 2
eISBN 978 1 83997 490 8

Printed and bound in Great Britain by CPI Group

Jessica Kingsley Publishers' policy is to use papers that are natural, renewable and recyclable
products and made from wood grown in sustainable forests. The logging and manufacturing
processes are expected to conform to the environmental regulations of the country of origin.

Jessica Kingsley Publishers
Carmelite House
50 Victoria Embankment
London EC4Y 0DZ

www.jkp.com

John Murray Press
Part of Hodder & Stoughton Limited
An Hachette UK Company

The authorised representative in the EEA is Hachette Ireland, 8 Castlecourt Centre,
Castleknock Road, Castleknock, Dublin 15, D15 YF6A, Ireland

Contents

Introduction

Understanding how relationships work, at home, school or in the wider world, is integral to the healthy development of all children. From exploring the concept of 'family' to looking at the complexities of friendship, this inclusive teaching and learning resource is based on the Department for Education (DfE) Relationships Education curriculum,[1] which is compulsory for all primary schools in England, but can be successfully taught to any children aged 7–11. This includes all-through and middle schools.

With a wealth of age-appropriate scenarios, quizzes, discussion-based activities and games aimed at engaging children in creative ways, these lesson plans enable educators to explore emotive topics like bullying and peer pressure, as well as the fun, security and comfort that healthy friendships provide.

Teaching Relationships Education in primary schools

Relationships play a key part in every child's life, from those at home to peer friendships and the wider relationships they may have at school, online or in the community.

Children should be encouraged to understand the reciprocal nature of healthy relationships and their rights and responsibilities within them. For most children, this starts with the relationships they have with primary caregivers, any siblings and wider family. As their experience of the world grows, children begin to realize that every family is different, from the culture and customs practised at home to the languages spoken, the food eaten and the household rules. Relationships Education aims to build empathy, promote equality and challenge all forms of discrimination, so that children grow up understanding and respecting the things that make everyone different.

Once children start to navigate relationships outside the home, social skills become paramount to making friends and communicating effectively both online and in the real world. From the sense of belonging and identity engendered by peer groups, to building the confidence to talk to adults, it is important that children understand the meaning of consent and how to set and maintain personal boundaries. This will help keep them

---

1 https://assets.publishing.service.gov.uk/media/62cea352e90e071e789ea9bf/Relationships_Education_RSE_and_Health_Education.pdf

THE POSITIVE RELATIONSHIPS CLASSROOM ACTIVITY BOOK

safe, able to manage conflict and resist negative peer pressure, building the foundations for healthy relationships in the future.

Mapped to the Relationships Curriculum

This book, divided into five chapters, provides classroom activities mapped against the DfE outcomes for Relationships Education (RE) in primary school using the Personal, Social, Health and Economic (PSHE) Association Programme of Study for PSHE education[2] as a framework. It is suitable for use with children aged 7–11, Lower Key Stage 2 (LKS2) and Upper Key Stage 2 (UKS2) in the United Kingdom (UK).

Chapter 1: All About Me

To meet the statutory guidance for teaching about relationships, the following topics in this chapter are drawn from across the curriculum to provide baseline learning:

- The knowledge that everyone is different, and the importance of respecting others.

- The importance of self-respect and how this links to their own happiness.

- The value of positive personal attributes, including honesty, integrity, courage, humility, kindness, generosity, thoughtfulness and trustworthiness.

- What personal boundaries are and how they might be used.

- How each person's body belongs to them, and the differences between appropriate and inappropriate or unsafe physical, and other, contact.

- How to ask for advice or help for themselves or others, and to keep trying until they are heard.

Chapter 2: Families and People Who Care for Me

To meet the statutory guidance for teaching about 'families and people who care for me' the following topics are covered:

- The importance of families for children growing up, because they can give love, security and stability.

- How stable, caring relationships, which may be of different types, are at the heart of happy families, and are important for children's security as they grow up.

- How families can look different but are all deserving of respect.

- How the characteristics of a healthy family life should include commitment,

---

2   https://pshe-association.org.uk/guidance/ks1-5/planning/long-term-planning

loyalty, protection and care and the importance of spending time together and sharing each other's lives.

- How to recognize if family relationships are making them feel unhappy or unsafe, and how to seek help or advice from others if needed.

Chapter 3: Caring Friendships

To meet the statutory guidance for teaching about the principles of caring friendships the following topics are covered (this includes online friendships as many children will already be using the internet and/or social media):

- The importance of friendships in making us feel happy and secure, and how people choose and make friends.

- The characteristics of friendships, including mutual trust and respect, truthfulness, loyalty, kindness, generosity, sharing interests and experiences, and support with problems and difficulties.

- What sorts of boundaries are appropriate in friendships with peers and others (including in a digital context).

- How healthy friendships are welcoming towards others, and do not exclude others or make them feel lonely.

- How most friendships have ups and downs and these can often be worked through so that the friendship is repaired or even strengthened; and that resorting to bullying or violence is never right.

- How to recognize who to trust and who not to trust, how to judge when a friendship is making them feel unhappy or uncomfortable, managing conflict, and where to go for help from others, if needed.

Chapter 4: Respectful Relationships

To meet the statutory guidance for teaching about respectful relationships the following topics are covered:

- The importance of respecting others, even when they are very different from them (e.g. physically, in character, personality or backgrounds), or make different choices or have different preferences or beliefs.

- Practical steps to take in a range of different contexts to improve or support respectful relationships.

- How in school and wider society they can expect to be treated with respect by others, and in turn they should show due respect to others.

- Different types of bullying (including cyberbullying), the impact of bullying, responsibilities of bystanders (primarily reporting bullying to an adult) and how to get help.

- What a stereotype is, and how stereotypes can be unfair, negative or destructive.

- The importance of consent in relationships with friends, peers and adults.

Chapter 5: Online Relationships and Being Safe

To meet the statutory guidance for teaching about online relationships and being safe the following topics are covered:

- How people can behave differently online, including pretending to be someone they are not.

- How the same principles apply to online relationships as to face-to-face relationships, including the importance of respect for others (including when we are anonymous).

- The rules and principles for keeping safe online, how to recognize risks, harmful content and contact, and how to report them.

- The concept of privacy and that it is not always right to keep secrets if they relate to being safe.

- How to respond safely and appropriately to unknown adults they may encounter (in all contexts, including online).

- How to recognize and report feelings of being unsafe or feeling bad about any adult.

- How to report concerns or abuse, and where to get advice (e.g. family, school or other sources).

Key vocabulary

At the start of each chapter is a box containing key vocabulary relating to the topics covered in the lesson plans. These are also mapped to the learning outcomes set in the RE Curriculum.[3]

While this book references the National Curriculum for Key Stage 2 in the UK, in the United States (US) these lesson plans are appropriate for teaching Elementary

---

3   For more information about statutory Relationships Education in primary school go to: www.gov.uk/government/publications/relationships-education-relationships-and-sex-education-rse-and-health-education/relationships-education-primary

children, in the second to fifth grades. Unlike the UK, Canada, Australia and India, the US has a decentralized educational system, meaning the content of the American or US Curriculum can be creative and flexible, varying state by state. This individuality reflects the ethos of this book, which is teaching children the importance of positive friendships and the value of family and family relationships, while developing personal qualities like respect, honesty, self-confidence and kindness.

Relationships Education could also be taught within the many co-curricular activities offered in American schools, teaching children learning for life, including critical thinking, communication and social skills.

Relationships Education policy

All primary schools in England are required to have a Relationships Education policy. While individual to the school, this will set out the subject content, how it is taught and who is responsible for teaching it.

Available free of charge on request, RE policies should be 'live' documents developed in consultation with staff, school governors, parents/carers and pupils.

Including parents and carers in Relationships Education

Parents/carers are encouraged to familiarize themselves with the contents of both the school RE policy and the RE curriculum to understand how it will be taught and when in the school year and so that they can prepare and support their children's learning at home. Examples of this collaborative approach can include inviting parents into school to review teaching materials, and hosting interactive RE workshops (online or in school).

While parents do not have the right to withdraw their children from RE, they are actively encouraged to give feedback, ask questions, voice concerns and share information.

Teaching about families in school

Central to teaching about families is the acknowledgement that they come in different shapes and sizes. This will be reflected in the school community so it is important for teachers to learn about their pupils in advance of delivering RE. For example, children may live with one or both biological parents, in a blended family, or with foster carers. Some will have same sex or transgender parents, and/or those who use different pronouns or prefer to be called something other than the traditional 'Mum' and 'Dad'. While the lesson plans in this book strive to be inclusive, by understanding the faith, culture and ethnic diversity of children in school, teachers can effectively adapt activities to reflect lived experience. For example, changing the names in scenarios, adapting role-plays to include different family dynamics or adding a faith perspective. This should mean that no child sits through a relationships lesson feeling isolated, unseen or unrepresented.

Children with care experience

RE can be particularly emotive for adopted children and those with care experience. For example, sharing birth stories or discussing family life can be especially triggering if a child is estranged from their biological parents. With the impact of adverse childhood experiences (ACEs)[4] and childhood trauma, including witnessing domestic abuse, now well documented, it is important that teachers work in a trauma-informed way so that they can plan accordingly.

To clarify, under the Children Act 1989,[5] a child is looked after by a local authority if they are in their care or provided with accommodation for more than 24 hours. This could be:

- a short-term voluntary placement (Section 20)

- living with foster carers (this could be a grandparent or other relative, known as a 'kinship placement')

- living in a residential children's home

- living in a residential school or secure unit.

Including foster carers, social workers and the child (where appropriate) in preparing for RE can help identify any potential trigger topics and agree a personal support strategy. Strategies could include the option to take time out if the child becomes overwhelmed or anxious, the amending of lesson plans to reflect different family make-ups or additional support at home if required. Acknowledging the beliefs and cultural heritage of birth families can help some children feel validated too.

How to use these lesson plans

Each chapter contains six complete lesson plans. These can be used as a whole, or if time is short, the contents can be mixed and matched to deliver individually or to enhance existing PSHE resources.

For each lesson, there is a warm-up to introduce the topic and test existing knowledge, activities to explore it in more detail and a review exercise to reinforce learning. Some extension activities have been suggested for individual lesson plans, but it is generally anticipated that at primary age, most learning will take place within a classroom environment with an adult educator to guide and support.

---

4   https://uktraumacouncil.org/research_practice/aces-research
5   Being accommodated under Section 20 Children Act 1989; or being made the subject of a Care Order under section 31 Children Act 1989.

Each lesson plan uses a wide range of teaching methods to meet the intended aims and learning outcomes. Interactive, creative and often solution focused, these include discussion-based tasks, case studies, role-play, problem-solving team games, quizzes and group work to develop the following skills and qualities considered central to healthy relationships:

- Communication.

- Confidence and assertiveness.

- Self-esteem and self-worth.

- Empathy and respect for others.

- Critical thinking and decision making.

- Recognizing and assessing potential risks.

- Managing conflict and coping with negative emotions.

- Knowing when to ask for help and where to go for support.

While it has not been possible to give detailed ideas and advice for adapting every exercise for those with special educational needs and disabilities (SEND), most activities offer alternative ideas for inclusive teaching.

Please note that copies of all worksheets, marked with [download symbol], can be photocopied and downloaded from https://library.jkp.com/redeem using the code EURRBQJ.

Signposting

Rather than writing a paragraph at the end of each lesson plan, it is anticipated that teachers will ensure that all children are informed where to go for help and support with any of the issues raised. Children should always be encouraged to talk to someone, usually a parental figure, but if this is not possible, a teacher or other trusted adult. Consider introducing the school safeguarding lead and any pastoral support leader during a lesson so that children know what help and support is available in school.

Also include signposting to local support services and referrals to statutory organizations, such as the Child and Adolescent Mental Health Service (CAMHS), as well as national charities and helplines, like Childline[6] or the NSPCC Helpline,[7] where children can ask questions via text, a chat box or phone line.

---

6   www.childline.org.uk
7   www.nspcc.org.uk/keeping-children-safe/reporting-abuse/nspcc-helpline

Confidentiality and safeguarding

The DfE document, 'Keeping children safe in education',[8] gives clear guidance on how to teach children to keep themselves and each other safe. There is also statutory guidance available for multi-agency working and safeguarding partnerships (e.g. education, social care and police), 'Working together to safeguard children'.[9]

Explain to the children what 'confidentiality' means and clarify the legal duty to report any safeguarding concerns. One way of explaining this is to say that information shared is confidential, unless it becomes clear that someone is at risk of being harmed or of harming others.

Preparing the environment

Try preparing for the behaviour you want by creating a relaxing environment in which to learn. Move things around within the classroom, change the lighting, use mood music or set up a quiet zone using comfy chairs, cushions or a rug for small group discussions to signal that RE is a safe space for learning. Consider beginning and ending each lesson with a circle time activity. Circles work well as everyone can see each other and there is no hierarchy, which should encourage more open conversations.

Collect together some simple props for role-play activities, such as hats and scarves, which can be used to help the children get into character, then quickly removed to signify coming out of it at the end. Consider using some warm-down techniques like 'shaking off' the role by vigorously shaking hands or feet (or both!) to help children move between the potentially emotive topics they are exploring through role-play and return to real life.

Boundaries

We all have lived experience but if you think children can learn from yours, use a distancing technique rather than telling the anecdote as a personal story. For example, present it as a scenario with questions for the children to work through: 'A child was anxious about telling an adult they were being bullied. Why do you think that might be?' This enables you to share what you learned to guide children who might be experiencing something similar, without overstepping the professional boundaries that are there to keep everyone safe.

Equally, sharing the learning without disclosing the details can work well; for example, 'Everyone feels anxious at some time. When I feel anxious it can really help me to talk to someone I trust, write my thoughts down, go for a walk and so on. Which of these might work for you?'

Finally, consider personal questions that may be asked and come up with some appropriate responses. While it is important that a child does not feel shamed or rejected for

---

8   www.gov.uk/government/publications/keeping-children-safe-in-education--2
9   www.gov.uk/government/publications/working-together-to-safeguard-children--2

asking, it is also an opportunity to demonstrate personal boundaries and the right to privacy in action.

Ground rules

It is important that RE is inclusive, so that all children feel valued, accepted and seen.

Devising a simple set of ground rules with the children can help set the boundaries and explain the meaning of confidentiality. Here is an example:

In this class:

- we are all different and worthy of respect

- we will speak one at a time

- we will actively listen to one another

- we will ask questions to help us learn

- we will keep things confidential unless they need to be shared to keep us/others safe

- we are kind to each other and ourselves.

These ground rules provide a basic behavioural contract, which can be referred to in the first instance should any rules be broken. If there is an incident, distinguish between the behaviour and the child. Basically, we can all change our behaviour but not ourselves, so be specific without making it feel like a personal attack. For example, 'When you talked over Paulo, I couldn't hear what he said. I'm going to ask him to repeat it so please remember to keep quiet and listen. If you want to talk after that we will listen to you.'

Asking questions

Some children may struggle to speak openly in the wider group. Others may live in a family where emotional topics are not discussed and asking questions is prohibited. To help resolve this, create other non-verbal ways to contribute, such as a question box or a question wall where children can leave notes to be responded to later on.

Evaluating learning

Make sure the children participate in the evaluation process so that they can assess their own learning and experiences as well as provide feedback for you. Suggested tools for evaluation include individual and group feedback, private reflection and self-evaluation, quizzes to reinforce learning and check out understanding.

Glossary

Below is a table of common terms, acronyms and words used throughout the book that it may be helpful to read about and become familiar with.

Age-appropriate	Suitable or right for the age a child is. Other factors like the child's maturity, cognitive and physical abilities may also be taken into account.
CAMHS	Child and Adolescent Mental Health Service
CSE	Child Sexual Exploitation
Culture	The customs, ideas and social behaviour of a particular group of people or society.
DfE	Department for Education
Ethnicity	Belonging to a group that has a common national or cultural tradition.
Equality	Ensuring that individuals, or groups of individuals, are not treated less favourably because of a protected characteristic. This includes race, gender, disability, belief or religion, sexual orientation, sex and age. This is legislated for in the Equality Act 2010.
Gender identity	The internal perception someone has of their gender and how they identify themselves.
KS2	Key Stage 2
LGBTQ+	This acronym is used as an inclusive term for those identifying as lesbian, gay, bisexual, transgender or questioning, plus any other non-heterosexuals.
Media	Online and traditional sources of news and information
Partner	Relationship partner of any gender
PSHE education	Personal, Social, Health and Economic education
RE	Relationships Education
Relationship	The way two or more people talk and behave towards each other.
RSE	Relationships and Sex Education
SEND	Special educational needs and disabilities
Sexual consent	The UK legal definition is that the individual must be over the age of 16 and able to understand the nature of the sex act and its consequences, there must be no pressure used, and they are able to communicate their decision to have sex.
Sexual orientation	The type of sexual, romantic and physical attraction someone feels for another person.
Social media	Websites and applications that enable users to create and share content or to participate in social networking (e.g. TikTok and Snapchat).
Stereotype	A commonly held belief about a person or group of people based on an assumption or incomplete knowledge, and then widely applied. This can lead to prejudice and discrimination.
Transgender	A broad term that can be used to describe people whose gender identity is different from the gender they were thought to be when they were born. 'Trans' is often used as shorthand for transgender.[10]

---

10 https://transequality.org/issues/resources/understanding-transgender-people-the-basics

CHAPTER 1

All About Me

KEY WORDS

Difference, trust, respect, kindness, honesty, self-esteem, self-worth, diversity and inclusion

LESSON 1: BOTTLE FISH

Aim

This is a creative way for children to represent themselves using recycled plastic bottles and craft materials. It aims to demonstrate diversity and inclusion in a visual way.

Learning outcomes

- Understand that everyone is different but of equal value.

- Know that individuals come together to form communities.

Time: 90 minutes (plus extra drying time)

Resources

- Paper

- Art supplies (coloured pencils, felt tip and marker pens)

- Empty 2 litre plastic bottles (clear where possible), complete with screw-top lids

- PVA glue and recycled plastic pots (to put the glue in)

- Coloured tissue paper, sequins, glitter and so on

- Acrylic paint (to stick to the plastic bottle) and brushes

- Newspaper (or large sheets of scrap paper to cover tables and dry painted craft material on)

- Art overalls or large t-shirts (to protect clothes)

- Sticky tape and scissors

- 1p and 2p coins

- Coloured card (to cut out eyes and fins)

- Access to the internet to show pictures of shoals of fish/goldfish (optional)

- Fishing line or clear nylon thread (to hang the fish from)

How to do it
Introduction (20 mins)

1. Invite the children to demonstrate with a show of hands if they have ever seen goldfish in a tank, pond or bowl. Then give out paper and ask them to draw one. This should have as much detail as possible and when finished, be given a name. Ask the children to introduce their goldfish to those sitting close by and finally, on the count of three, to hold their pictures above their heads. Comment that although they are all pictures of goldfish, each one is different and unique.

2. If you have online pictures of shoals of fish or videos to reinforce this sentiment, show the children now.

Activity 1 (60 minutes)

1. Explain that the class is going to create its own shoal of 'rainbow' fish. These will be made and designed by the children to reflect their personality, likes and dislikes – in fact, everything that makes them special and unique, just like the goldfish.

2. Give each child a plastic bottle with the lid screwed on.

3. To make the body of the fish, hold the bottleneck and scrunch it like a concertina down three quarters of the bottle, leaving the last quarter in its original form. Hold the concertinaed plastic in place by wrapping sticky tape around it several times.

4. To make the tail, first carefully cut the end of the bottle off. Then cut lots of straight lines 2cm apart up to the line created by the sticky tape, being extra careful as the plastic strips can be sharp. To prevent the plastic splitting any further add one more circle of sticky tape, then fluff the tassels out to create a fish tail effect.

5. It is now time to decorate and personalize the fish. Invite the children to consider colours and shapes that they think represent who they are, both their outer and inner self. Tear bits of coloured tissue paper, dip them in glue and apply them to the bottle to create a pattern. Show how tissue paper can be layered to make new colours, holding it up to the light to see the effect created. Leave to dry thoroughly.

6. While the body is drying, instruct the children to paint the bottle top, which will become the fish's mouth, then leave it on newspaper to dry.

7. When every part of the fish is thoroughly dry, it is ready to be decorated with sequins, glitter or scraps of sparkly fabric so that the fish gleam in the light. Make fish eyes by first drawing around a 2p coin twice on white

card and cutting the circles out, then taking a 1p coin and repeating on black card. There should now be four circles of card, two of each colour. Glue the black circles onto the middles of the white ones and then glue the 'eyes' on either side of the head.

8. Complete by making two identical fins out of thin card. These can be any size or shape, decorated or plain, but they need to be big enough to comfortably fold over 1.5cm at the bottom without ruining the design. This area will be spread with glue and the fins stuck to the fish, one at the top and one at the bottom.

9. Once everything has dried, create a class display by making a small hole in the top fin of each fish, threading through fishing line or invisible thread and then pinning or stapling to the ceiling. Hang the fish at different lengths to create a class shoal of fish, where everyone swims together in the same direction.

Review (10 minutes)

1. Invite the children in turn to introduce their fish, explaining things that makes them different to other fish on display, and things that are the same.

2. Conclude that the shoal of fish they have created is representative of the diversity in the class and the unique qualities of the children that made them – all similar and of equal value, but ultimately all different too.

Extension activity

Consider creating a whole underwater scene for the fish to swim in, for example making seaweed by using strips of green tissue paper decorated with different scraps of sparkly materials.

LESSON 2: EXPLORING IDENTITY

Aim

This lesson helps children explore the concept of identity, their own and those of others, before creating a visual representation.

Learning outcomes

- Recognize differences and similarities in identities.

- Understand that identities are made up of different characteristics.

- Understand that identity, including heritage, faith and culture, should be respected and difference celebrated.

Time: 80 minutes

Resources

- Whiteboard and pens

- Sets of the Activity 2: Identity Cards (one set per group of four to six children)

- Pre-cut triangles of stiff paper for bunting (make by cutting 20cm squares diagonally in half)

- Art supplies (coloured pencils, felt tip and marker pens)

- String or ribbon (to staple the paper triangles to)

- A stapler and drawing pins (to hang the bunting after completion)

How to do it
Introduction (10 minutes)

1. Facilitate a circle time exercise, inviting each child to describe themselves in one sentence.

2. Keep a simple tally on the whiteboard of how many children describe themselves in terms of physical features and how many describe skills or a personal quality. It is likely that the majority describe how they look, which

is only part of an identity. Explain that in the next activity they are going to learn about other things that make a person who they are.

Activity 1 (30 minutes)

1. Divide into groups of four to six, giving each group a set of Activity 2: Identity Cards. Their task is to first discuss and agree if the description on a card is part of someone's identity and if so, rank them as:

   ▨ very important

   ▨ quite important

   ▨ not important at all.

2. Suggest they create three piles to share and compare later back in the wider class.

3. Decisions are likely to vary, so spend time exploring why. Suggest that identity is how you see yourself, so is complex and made up of lots of different things, which can change over time. For example, a child's identity may be linked to their family, school and friendship group whereas an adult's primary identity may be their job, such as being a doctor, teacher or hairdresser. Identity can also include things like gender, marital status and parenthood.

Teaching tip: This discussion provides an opportunity to talk about gender identity and sexuality in an age-appropriate way.

Activity 2 (30 minutes)

1. Summarize that everyone's identity is unique. To celebrate this, the children are going to make a string of 'identity bunting' representing the diversity within the class.

2. Set up tables with craft materials and blank triangles to decorate, encouraging the children to talk and share information about their heritage as they work. As bunting can be seen from different angles, they will need to plan their designs to decorate both sides of the triangle using words, shapes, symbols and pictures. Stress that apart from making sure their name is on there, it is for them to decide which parts of their identity to include.

3. Once everyone has at least one fully decorated triangle, begin stapling them equal distance along the length of string or ribbon. Consider inviting classroom staff to create their own too.

4. Hang the bunting, then stand back and review with the children so that they can fully appreciate and celebrate the unique identities in the class.

Review (10 minutes)

1. Return to a seated circle, again inviting each child to share one thing about their own identity and one thing they have learned about the identity of another member of the class. Recap that identity is based on so much more than just physical attributes, to include values, beliefs and achievements, along with social and cultural identities that help us identify each other. Stress that no single identity is better, they are all just different, and that everyone has the right to be respected for who they are.

Extension activity

Consider asking every child in the school to make an identity triangle. These can be put together with the class ones to celebrate the diversity of identities within the whole school community.

ACTIVITY 2: IDENTITY CARDS

The colour of
your hair

What time
you get up

Your faith
or religion

The second
letter of your
last name

The food
you eat

How you
describe your
ethnicity

Your shoe
size

How tall
you are

Which subjects
you enjoy
at school

The languages you speak	**The names of your best friends**	**Where you were born**
How old you are	**The colour of your eyes**	**If you have a lucky number**
Where you live	**Things that make you laugh**	**Your personality**

The music
you like

Your gender

Your favourite
colour

The holidays
you celebrate

Your favourite
game

The sports team
you support

The clothes
you wear

The school
you go to

Your hairstyle

LESSON 3: KINDNESS MIRRORS

Aim
This activity builds confidence and increases self-esteem by encouraging children to be kind to themselves and others, focusing on personal strengths and positive attributes.

Learning outcomes

- Understand the meaning of random kindness and how to practise it.

- Recognize personal strengths and understand the skills and qualities valued by others.

- Understand how being kind to yourself and self-validation can increase confidence and raise self-esteem.

Time: 100 minutes

Resources

- Scissors

- Sheets of coloured light craft foam (to cut out petal shapes from)

- Paper plates

- Small circular mirrors (one for each child)

- PVA glue

- Art supplies (coloured pencils, felt tip and marker pens)

- String, scissors and gaffer tape (or similar)

Teaching tip: Consider making a simple petal shape template so they are all the same. If you are working with younger children, you could also cut the petals out in advance.

How to do it
Introduction (10 minutes)

1. Read out this statement:

     To love others, you have to love yourself.

2. Facilitate a short discussion that considers what the children think this means and how true they think the statement is. Clarify that loving yourself isn't the same as being conceited, it is about recognizing and feeling comfortable with your own strengths and positive qualities, which builds confidence and a sense of self-worth. Suggest that if you can appreciate your own strengths, you are more likely to set achievable goals and be kinder to yourself if/when things go wrong, and be ready to try again.

Activity 1 (20 minutes)

1. Ask the children, working in pairs, to remember:

   ▣ the last time they did a random act of kindness for a family member

   ▣ the last time they did something kind for someone outside the home

   ▣ the last time they were kind to themselves.

2. Allow five minutes for the children to share examples, then bring the whole class back together.

3. Write on the whiteboard the headings, 'Family', 'Others' and 'Self' and invite the children to call out examples of random kindness they heard and found inspiring from their conversations.

4. Explain that a random kindness can be big or small; it is about the act of giving rather than what is given. For example, doing a chore without being asked, paying someone a compliment or holding a door open are all simple things to do that can mean a lot to others.

5. Move on to consider self-kindness, asking again for inspiring examples. Children are often less confident talking about this, not wanting to confuse it with being selfish or self-indulgent. For example, giving someone the last chocolate biscuit is kind, but if you take it for yourself, it's selfish rather than self-kindness. Clarify that being kind to yourself is a form of self-care that includes not using harsh words about yourself, holding yourself to impossibly high standards or punishing yourself if things go wrong, which can all damage self-esteem and confidence. Being kind to yourself in simple terms means treating yourself with the same care and respect that you would treat others, recognizing the things you are good at and appreciating your positive qualities.

Activity 2 (15 minutes)

1. Instruct the children to walk around the room, stopping when you clap your hands to give the person nearest them a positive comment. The compliment

should be received by smiling and saying, 'Thank you' before offering a compliment back.

2. Keep going until everyone has experienced giving and receiving at least six positive comments.

3. Review how it feels to give and receive positive comments. Suggest that being able to recognize the positive attributes we all have can help improve confidence and self-worth, which in turn can build resilience to cope with less positive experiences.

Activity 3 (45 minutes)

1. Introduce the next activity, which focuses on self-love and giving and receiving positive comments. Seat the children in small groups around tables with the craft equipment laid out. Give everyone a round mirror. These should be stuck in the middle of the paper plate. Alternatively, if you don't have mirrors, ask the young people to draw a self-portrait in the middle of the paper plate using coloured pens.

2. Instruct each child to cut out six same-size coloured petals from the craft foam, plus one extra petal in a contrasting colour.

3. On the extra petal, ask the children to write this reminder: 'Be kind to yourself.' They should then proceed to write something positive about themselves on each of the other petals, and decorate it. When all the petals are complete, demonstrate how to arrange the petals around the mirror to form a flower, then glue them down.

4. If there are children not used to positive affirmations or who lack confidence, this may take some time, so be ready to support and provide ideas. Once done, ask everyone to cut out a petal for each child on their table. On this they should write things they like, admire or respect about that person, to contribute to their Kindness Mirror.

5. Leave to dry thoroughly, then turn over. Hang the mirrors by cutting a small length of string, folding it in half to create a hook and then sticking it in the top rim of the plate with gaffer tape. These are now ready to hang and display somewhere the children can easily be reminded of all their positive skills and qualities whenever they look in the mirror.

Review (10 minutes)

1. Ask the children to choose a new partner to discuss ideas for being kind to yourself, now that they have explored the meaning of self-kindness and self-love and experienced the power of positive comments.

2. Invite the children to share those they think are the most inspiring and/or creative with the wider group.

3. Finally, task the children with doing one act of self-kindness a day for themselves as well as one act of random kindness for others for two weeks. They should record these to share and compare in class time, reflecting on the power of kindness.

Extension activity

Consider setting this as a whole school pledge, suggesting that random acts of kindness can increase confidence, build communication skills and make individuals feel more positive, as well as improving the community culture too.

LESSON 4: COLOUR MY FEELINGS

Aim

The activities in this lesson introduce the idea of using colour as a way for children to name their emotions and express how they feel.

Learning outcomes

- Understand that all feelings are normal and valid.

- Know that colours can be associated with emotions as a way to express how you feel without using words.

- Understand that everyone has feelings and can respond differently.

Time: 50 minutes

Resources

- Whiteboard and marker pens

- Sticky notes and pens

- A6 sheets of drawing quality paper (six sheets per child)

- Art supplies (coloured pencils, felt tip and marker pens)

- Clear wall space (the finished work will be displayed here later)

- Six A4 sheets of paper titled 'Happy', 'Sad', 'Excited', 'Angry', 'Anxious' and 'Calm'

- Colour diaries (optional)

How to do it
Introduction (5 minutes)

1. Explain that there are no 'good' or 'bad' emotions, we all experience a wide range of feelings in response to the life experiences we have. Ask the children to call out the names of different feelings and emotions, recording them on a whiteboard as you go along.

   Teaching tip: Adapt this to a visual exercise by printing off a series of emoji images, each showing a different emotion. In a circle, give one to each child, inviting them to guess which emotion the picture is portraying. If they get it wrong or don't know, invite the rest of the class to guess.

Activity 1 (15 minutes)

1. Explain that you are going to call out a series of colours (red, blue, yellow etc.) after which the children should quickly write down on a sticky note any feeling or emotion that springs to mind when they hear it.

2. Share and compare after each round. Stress that colour association is personal, so there is no right or wrong answer as everyone is unique and therefore experiences things differently. Suggest that colour is sometimes used in conversation to convey moods, for example someone saying they 'see red' when they are angry. It is also used creatively in things like song lyrics, for example 'feeling blue'.

Activity 2 (20 minutes)

1. Building on this idea, prepare the room for working in groups of four to six, with a pack of coloured pens and a stack of A6 paper on each table. Create a display area, sticking the six A4 title sheets on the wall at a distance to each other to create 'emotion zones'.

2. Suggest that as well as attaching feelings to colours, some people use colour as a way of exploring their own emotions and showing others how they feel. Being able to use colours like this can help if you are feeling something but do not have the words to express it. It can also help identify 'triggers' for emotions and from there develop strategies to cope when feelings threaten to overwhelm or are leading to a pattern of behaviour that is unhelpful.

3. To try this out, select a wide range of emotions and feelings from those suggested by the children earlier and read them aloud off the whiteboard. After each one, the children should take a sheet of paper and fill it with one or more colours to represent how that emotion feels to them. Demonstrate painting different densities of paint to represent depth of feeling and also layering to create new colours. Keep the activity going at a pace that prompts a swift response but enough time to colour in the whole sheet. Three to five minutes per round is usually sufficient.

4. After each round, invite the children to hold up their paper to compare the colours the emotion provokes. Comment on similarity and differences; for example, has everyone filled their 'angry' paper with red, a colour tradition-ally associated with anger, or does another colour signify anger for them? Point out that many people think red reflects feelings of love, warmth and

comfort. Invite the children to talk with a partner about why they chose the colours and come up with some other examples, which they can share back in the bigger group.

Review (10 minutes)

1. Invite everyone to stick their sheets of paper on the display wall, under the correct header, to create a feelings wall.

2. Remind the children that we all experience a wide range of emotions and feelings every day, and that colour is just one way of expressing them. Suggest that talking about how you feel with someone you trust is important too and can help build coping skills to manage challenges in life.

Extension activity

Encourage the children to keep a mood colour diary, where they keep a note of their changing emotions throughout each day, using colour. This can be done over a weekend or week and then used to explore situations and experiences that trigger feelings of happiness, anger and so on. From here, each child can consider personal strategies for doing more of the things that bring positive feelings, and ways to manage those that are more challenging.

LESSON 5: POSITIVE AFFIRMATION CARDS

Aim

For children to interpret a series of motivational statements and then create their own Positive Affirmation Card to inspire themselves and others.

Learning outcomes

- Understand the importance of positive self-image.

- Understand that words are powerful and can be linked to feelings and inspire actions.

- Learn the concept of positive affirmations and how to use them.

Time: 55 minutes

Resources

- Sets of the Activity 1: Self-Love Statements (one per group of four children)

- A5 card or stiff paper (one per child)

- Handwriting pens

- Paper (to practise designing their card on)

- Arts and craft materials (to decorate the cards)

- Wall space (or a display board)

How to do it
Introduction (10 minutes)

1. Ask if any of the children can give a definition of the term 'self-love' and what they think it means and why it is important for emotional wellbeing and good mental health.

2. Conclude that self-love includes treating yourself with respect and recognizing your strengths, while being honest with yourself when setting goals and being kind if you struggle. In short, self-love is having a healthy relationship with yourself. Explain that while not everybody is born with

it, self-love can be developed to help you be your best self. You can also support and encourage self-love in others.

Activity 1 (15 minutes)

1. Divide the class into groups of four, giving each group a set of Activity 1: Self-Love Statements. On them are ten different positive statements related to self-love. The task is to read and discuss what they think each one means.

2. Once they have done this, invite each group in turn to share the key points of their discussion about one of the cards. Afterwards check in with the others to see if their group had similar or different ideas about what it meant to them.

Activity 2 (15 minutes)

1. Give each child an A5 piece of card and explain they are going to design their own 'Affirmation Card' to motivate and inspire other children to be proud of who they are. Examples:

   'You are strong.'

   'Keep going, you can do it.'

   'Be kind to yourself.'

   'You are unique and special.'

2. Give out plain paper and pens to write drafts on. Once they are happy with their final statement, they can write it in the middle of the A5 card, and then decorate using the arts and craft materials.

Review (15 minutes)

1. Invite each child to the front of the class to read out their new Affirmation Card, leading a round of applause after each child has read.

2. Display all of the Affirmation Cards together to create a 'Wall of Self-Love' to motivate and inspire everyone. Conclude that believing in yourself and your abilities can help you feel more confident and motivated to try new things, overcome challenges and work towards achievable goals.

ACTIVITY 1: SELF-LOVE STATEMENTS

Be your own
best friend

Be a flower;
learn and grow

Talk to and
about yourself
with kindness

Be brave,
be confident,
be you

Just be
yourself. The
real thing
is so much
better than
a copy

You are enough,
just as you are

Self-
confidence
comes from
within. No
one can 'give'
it to you

LESSON 6: POSITIVE SELF-TALK

Aim
To introduce children to the concept of positive 'self-talk' to build confidence in their abilities and achievements as well as build resilience to cope with future challenges.

Learning outcomes

- Understand that positive self-talk can impact on how you feel, think and behave, increasing motivation and making it more likely to overcome challenges and reach goals.

- Understand that negative self-talk has the opposite effect, reinforcing negative thoughts and beliefs, damaging self-esteem and confidence and potentially impacting on actions.

Time: 80 minutes

Resources

- Whiteboard, marker pens and a timer

- Hula hoops (two per team of eight children)

- Copies of the Activity 3: Positive Self-Talk Scenarios

- Seats (for the role-play activity)

How to do it
Introduction (5 minutes)

1. Start by acknowledging that sometimes things go wrong or are difficult. Explain that while life's up and downs are normal, learning the skills to cope and overcome challenges can help you bounce back quicker, ready to try again. Suggest that engaging in positive self-talk, using words of encouragement and cheering yourself on can help, rather than getting into a spiral of negative self-talk, telling yourself you will fail, or the worst will happen.

Activity 1 (15 minutes)

1. Read the following scenario to illustrate meaning and facilitate a discussion using the prompt questions. The idea is to explore how Sam might feel and how using positive or negative self-talk might impact on thoughts, feelings and behaviour.

SCENARIO

Sam has been chosen to take the penalty for their football team. Sam feels really nervous and a bit scared. Winning the match depends on this, it is a big moment.

Negative self-talk: 'Why did they choose me? I bet I miss this penalty, I always miss. Then everyone will hate me and blame me for losing the match…'

Positive self-talk: 'This penalty is important, so it is normal to feel anxious, but that won't stop me doing my best. I will focus on the goal and where I want the ball to go, then take the shot. I can do this; I know I can!'

Prompt questions:

1. What might Sam be thinking while waiting to take the penalty?

2. How might Sam feel?

3. How will this help/hinder taking the penalty shot? How might it affect Sam's performance in the rest of the match?

4. How might Sam think, feel and behave afterwards, whether a winning goal is scored or not?

For example, negative self-talk could trigger negative thoughts about their ability, reinforcing the feeling of not being good enough. Even if Sam does score, negative self-talk could leave them believing that scoring is down to luck rather than skill. This could affect how they play for the rest of the match and even discourage them from playing for the team again.

2. Conclude that Sam may or may not score the penalty that wins the match, but using positive self-talk can help calm anxiety and focus thoughts so they feel better prepared to take the shot. The resilience built through positive self-talk should also make it easier to cope with the disappointment if Sam does miss, motivating them to resume football training ready to try again next time, rather than giving up.

Activity 2 (20 minutes)

1. Use this game (or a similar one) to demonstrate the effect of positive and negative self-talk on completing a team challenge. Divide the children into teams of eight, instructing each team to hold hands and form a circle. Gently break the handclasp of two children and hang a hula-hoop on one arm before re-joining the hands.

2. Explain that the challenge is to pass the hula-hoop around the circle as fast as possible without talking and without unclasping hands. They can do this by each child stepping through the hula-hoop with the support and co-operation of their teammates, but the children will need to work this out for themselves.

3. Call out 'Go!' to start the challenge, and time how long it takes for each group to complete it. Record the times up on a whiteboard and then allow the children a two-minute team talk to discuss how they can improve their performance to complete the challenge faster. Ask each team to set a time goal for next time and record this in a different colour alongside their previous one.

4. Before they try again, ask teams to sit in a circle and take it in turns to pass the message, 'I can't do this any faster', around the circle ten times. Encourage them to be emphatic in the statement, shaking their heads as they say it, getting louder each time so the negativity fills the room. Immediately after the tenth time, call 'Go!' to re-do the challenge, again timing each group to completion. Without comment, write up the new times next to the goal each team set for improvement.

5. Then repeat, using positive self-talk in the team circle instead. This time, encourage the children to cheer themselves on, like a coach, loudly declaring, 'I can do this, I am fast!' ten times before their final attempt to complete the task and improve their score.

6. Record the time it takes each team, which should show an improvement bringing it closest to or even exceeding the goal set. Encourage each team to congratulate each other on both their individual and team performances.

7. Afterwards, ask each team to reflect on how motivated and ready to take on a challenge they felt after the negative self-talk. Did it make a difference? Move on to review the positive self-talk experience, again reflecting on feelings and any motivation this created to try harder for the team. Does telling yourself you can do something make a difference?

8. Finish on a positive note by asking each child in turn, 'Can you achieve your goals?' to which they should shout the reply, 'Yes, I can!'

Activity 3 (30 minutes)

1. The next part of the lesson aims to consolidate the learning so far as the children work in threes to role-play the Activity 3: Positive Self-Talk Scenarios, which feature people who need to make a choice or decision.

2. For each scenario, one child should sit on a seat and assume the character of the decision-maker. The other two children will also play that character, but they will be the internal doubts, fears or anxieties the person is having about making the decision or choice. It is their job to stand either side of the seat loudly whispering negative self-talk to try and influence the decision that the character will make at the end of three minutes. The decision-maker should listen to the negative voices but also challenge and question them aloud using positive self-talk.

3. Call time and ask each seated child, still in character, to tell the rest of their group the choice or decision they are making.

4. Instruct all of the children to stand up, shake off their assumed characters, and then spend a couple of minutes reviewing how it felt to both give and receive negative self-talk, the effect it had on decision-making and how easy or hard it was to challenge negative voices with positive self-talk.

5. Then change scenarios and swap roles until each child has experienced giving and receiving both types of self-talk at least once.

Review (10 minutes)

1. Bring everyone back together to review what has been learned from the lesson using these prompt questions:

   ▢ Which is more powerful; positive or negative self-talk?

   ▢ If you only listen to negative self-talk, what is likely to happen?

   ▢ How could positive self-talk help in real life?

2. Suggest that constant negative self-talk can drown out the positive, reduce confidence and make people doubt their abilities and strengths.

3. Alternatively, supporting and coaching yourself using positive self-talk can increase confidence and the motivation to keep going, even when things get tough.

Extension activity

Consider making pledges or creating action plans for using positive self-talk in specific situations, and then review progress.

ACTIVITY 3: POSITIVE SELF-TALK SCENARIOS

Scenario 1: You have written a poem you think is good. Your teacher agrees and asks you to read it out in class. You are not sure; what if the other children don't like poetry or laugh?

Scenario 2: Your sports coach is asking for volunteers to help with the younger team. You usually enjoy helping but none of your friends puts their hand up. Should you put yours up first?

Scenario 3: Your spelling test is on Friday. You have come top of the class for the last four weeks, now everyone is teasing you. Perhaps you should try less hard or pretend to do badly this week, so they stop?

ACTIVITY 3: POSITIVE SELF-TALK SCENARIOS

CHAPTER 2

Families and People Who Care for Me

KEY WORDS

Family, relationships, respect, love, care, security, commitment, diversity and difference

LESSON 1: MY FAMILY AND ME

Aim

The activities in this lesson explore family and individual identity to learn more about and celebrate the different cultural, ethnic and family roots within the class.

Learning outcomes

- Understand that names can have meaning and history, both personal, familial and cultural.

- Know that different elements make a family unique and special.

- Recognize how family identify, past and present, can shape personal identity.

Time: 100 minutes (plus drying time)

Resources

- Information about the history of family coats of arms (e.g. www.college-of-arms.gov.uk)

- Internet access, computer and printer

- Paper and pens

- Pre-prepared wooden planks. Do this using recycled pallets taken apart so that there is a plank for each child. Take out any nails or staples and make sure the wood is clean and dry. Roughly paint with dark wood stain or a dark coloured matt paint and leave to dry.

- Sticks of white chalk

- Pencils

- Sticky tape

- Chalk paint pens (fine and thick nib)

- Clear varnish and brushes

Teaching tip: If time is short, consider taking large cardboard boxes apart and using the recycled card, cut into lengths, instead of recycled wooden planks.

How to do it
Introduction (10 minutes)

1. Ask the children if they know what a coat of arms or a family motto is. Listen to suggestions, informing the children that historically a coat of arms was made up of eight distinctive images[1] to form a unique design to go on the shields of medieval knights. It then became popular with wealthy families who wanted their own, designed by a special 'heraldic' artist, using images to represent the family's achievements, wealth and status, often with a family motto written underneath. These coats of arms have now been passed down through many generations and tell us about a family's history, their identity. To be officially recognized, a coat of arms must be registered with the College of Arms,[2] which is the heraldic authority for England, Wales, Northern Ireland and much of the Commonwealth, including Australia and New Zealand. Well-known examples include the coats of arms belonging to different members of the Royal family, which can be seen on any product they endorse, including food items like honey, biscuits and chocolate.

2. While not every family has an 'official' coat of arms, there are lots of companies that offer to design them in a traditional style, which can be printed on everything from tea towels to vintage looking plaques to hang on a wall.

3. Share the selection you have prepared, asking the children to look in detail to inspire them to create their own later on in the lesson.

Activity 1 (20 minutes)

1. Suggest that one thing commonly found on a coat of arms is a symbol or image that represents the history of the family name. For example, 'Smith', which is reputedly the most common surname in the UK, originates from the Old English word 'Smit' which means to strike or to hit, used to describe a blacksmith (someone who works with metal). Therefore, a family coat of arms designed for the Smith family may include a blacksmith hammer to represent this.

2. Task the children to work in pairs with paper and pens to make notes and conduct some online research to establish what their family name means or where it originates from.

3. Bring the class back together to share their findings.

---

1 www.historylearningsite.co.uk/coats_of_arms_heraldry.htm
2 www.college-of-arms.gov.uk/services/granting-arms

4. Inform the children that in many ancient cultures people believed that names have power. Because of this, as well as having a family name, babies were often named after gods or goddesses (or names derived from them) with attributes their parents or carers valued, perhaps hoping they would have these too, or as a charm to keep them safe through life.

5. Suggest that in modern culture, choosing a first name is still very important and often the choice has a story or reason behind it as well as simply being a name the decision-maker likes. For example:

   ▣ a traditional family name or named in memory of a family member

   ▣ a faith-based name

   ▣ a name of a favourite song

   ▣ a name of a favourite movie star or sporting hero

   ▣ a name of a place with significant meaning to the name giver

   ▣ a name of a season (e.g. Summer).

Activity 2 (15 minutes)

1. Once everyone has completed the task of asking about the origin of their name or names, facilitate a circle time exercise where each child says their name and shares something about how they came to have it, for example why it was chosen: 'My name is Lena, which is a popular girl's name in Poland where I was born. I was named after my father's younger sister.'

2. After everyone has spoken, say a collective thank you for sharing. Suggest that names are an important part of your identity and contribute to developing your sense of self. They can also carry a sense of home, identity and links to family or culture.

Activity 3 (45 minutes)

1. This activity brings together learning from the previous two exercises, making a wooden sign to celebrate identity by designing a coat of arms and a family motto.

2. With the children working in groups around tables set up with the art supplies required for the task, ask each child to design a coat of arms for their family, based on their research, and a short sentence to describe their family. This will be their family motto. Each one will be different as it is for individuals to choose what has meaning and importance to them but will need to fit onto the pre-prepared pallet planks which will hang vertically when finished.

3. Once the coat of arms is designed and the outline drawn onto a sheet of paper, the children can choose a typeface for their family mottos, write them in a Word document and then print them off. Next in a new document, using the same font or a different one, they should write their name and print this off too. Instruct the children to take a piece of chalk and scribble thickly over the back of each sheet of paper making sure that all of their designs are covered, similar to using tracing paper.

4. Give each child a pallet plank, checking once more to make sure there are no nails left in it.

5. Turning the plank so it is portrait, tell them to arrange their designs chalk-side down so that their name is at the top, the coat of arms is in the middle with the family motto underneath. Use sticky tape to keep everything in place, then firmly trace in pencil over the top hard enough to leave a chalk imprint on the wood. Check by looking under a small section at a time, being careful to stick it back in the same place. When complete, remove all the paper.

6. Outline the design with a fine chalk paint marker and leave to dry. Use a damp cloth to remove any chalk residue, then colour in the family coat of arms and the rest of the letters in coloured chalk paint markers. Additional decorative symbols, pictures or signs related to the family can be added before leaving to dry. Use clear varnish to 'seal' the paint and prevent damage and leave for at least 24 hours to completely dry.

7. Display the wooden planks hung vertically together to form a wall representing the family identity of all the children in the class.

Review (10 minutes)

1. Facilitate gallery time so that the children can learn more about each other. Suggest that just as historic family coats of arms and mottos told us about families of the past, the planks the children have designed tell us about the diversity and rich culture of their families today. This sense of family and tradition helps shape individual identity and gives us a sense of who we are.

Extension activity

Task the children with finding out more about the origin of their first name(s) from parents/carers and wider family. This can be their given name, a shortened version, or another name they are known by. Information gathered can be shared back in the classroom at a later date.

LESSON 2: FAMILIES AND THOSE WHO CARE FOR ME

Aim

This lesson explores the meaning of family. It includes a craft-based activity to help children celebrate the diversity of those who care for them.

Learning outcomes

- Understand that everyone has a unique network of relationships made up of people we live with in families, wider family, distant connections.

- Understand that family networks come in different shapes and sizes, all of which are normal.

- Recognize that some people are emotionally closer and more important to us than others.

Time: 100 minutes

Resources

- Large sheets of paper

- Square blank canvases (approximately 30cm x 30cm)

- String, glue spreaders and PVA glue

- Art supplies (pencils, felt tip and marker pens, paint and brushes)

- Beads, seeds and sequins

Teaching tip: If time is short, use sheets of stiff card instead of canvas and decorate with felt pens and markers only.

How to do it
Introduction (10 minutes)

1. Start by asking the children to call out what they think the word 'family' means, recording ideas and leading a discussion that explores the different types of families, for example birth families, foster and adoptive families, people in the community who are like family. Acknowledge each suggestion,

making the point that families are likely to change over time due to life events (births, deaths, marriages etc.) and that everyone's family network looks different.

Activity 1 (20 minutes)

1. Explain that a 'family tree', sometimes called a genealogy chart or family map, is a visual representation of family relationships. This includes names, birth dates, marriages, deaths, going back generations and sometimes, moving across continents as people travelled and formed new branches.

2. The task for the children is to create their own family tree to represent the people they live with now, and their home. This may include biological relatives as well as other adults who care for them.

3. Give everyone a large sheet of paper. Starting in pencil, instruct them to draw the outline of a large tree that fills the sheet of paper. Once they have the drawing, they can go over the outline in pen and erase the pencil lines. Their personal 'family tree' is now ready to be decorated using the following key:

   ▨ Roots = My heritage (where my family/I come from)

   ▨ Trunk = Me (what makes me unique)

   ▨ Branches = People in my family

   ▨ Leaves = Things we like doing together

4. When complete, ask each child to introduce their tree, either to the whole class or in small groups. Remind them that just as each family is unique, the trees will all be different too. Encourage questions and take opportunities to discuss how family and home contributes to a sense of who you are, an identity.

Activity 2: (60 minutes, including drying time)

1. This craft activity moves on to explore family and other important relationships. Give each child a blank canvas and instruct them to lightly draw in pencil a small heart shape in the middle. This should be labelled, 'Me'. Around this they should draw three concentric hearts, big enough to fill the canvas. The first heart represents 'Those closest to me', the second 'My wider family' and the outer heart 'Other people who care for me'.

2. Taking the string and using a brush and PVA glue, demonstrate to the children how to curl and stick it around the perimeter of each of the heart shapes to create a raised ridge and define the different relationship zones.

3. Once the string has thoroughly dried, invite the children to choose a different colour to paint each relationship section of the heart. They paint the inside heart first and work outwards to avoid smudging, although the string boarder should prevent any colour bleeding from one area to another. Again, leave to dry thoroughly.

4. Next, ask the children to choose a bead, seed or sequin to represent themselves, then glue it into the central heart. This shows them as central to all the different relationships they have. After that they can populate each of the different areas with the key people in their life, again choosing a bead, seed or sequin to represent each one. Then, using a marker pen, the children can write a family message around the outside of the largest heart, following the curves of the shape. Display the canvases together to create a Family Wall.

Review (10 minutes)

1. Facilitate gallery time where the children can introduce their collage and some of their relationships that mean a lot to them. Reinforce the message that families are diverse and that there is no such thing as a 'normal' family. They are all unique, like the people who are in them, and that this is something to celebrate.

LESSON 3: DIFFERENT FAMILIES

Aims

This lesson the children explore different relationships that can make a family before creating their own family portrait to raise awareness about difference and similarities.

Learning outcomes

- Understand that all families have some things the same and some different.

- Recognize that positive family relationships are based on love, care, support, respect and trust.

- Understand that families are different sizes and are made up of different people.

- Recognize that families enjoy spending time together in different ways.

Time: 105 minutes

Resources

- Pictures of different family structures (e.g. single parents, same gender parents, biracial parents, foster families). For the purposes of this activity, these need to include at least one baby, child or teenager

- Paper

- Sticky labels

- Lollipop sticks

- Circles of white card (pre-cut using the template of a 2p for adults and 10p for children)

- Art supplies (drawing pencils, felt tips, paints and brushes)

- Craft materials (scissors, material, wool, fake fur, glitter, sequins etc.)

- A3 pieces of card

- Glue

How to do it
Introduction (10 minutes)

1. Facilitate a quick circle time based on word association where each child offers a word to describe their family. Repeat until ideas have been exhausted.

2. Reflect on the diversity of words used, concluding that all families are different.

Activity 1 (20 minutes)

1. Working in small groups, give the children a picture of a family, and some paper and pencils. Explain that their task is to create an imaginary profile of this family, from the perspective of a child seen in the photo, ending with the sentence, 'Together, we are all a family'. This should include:

   ▫ the names of each family member

   ▫ the relationships they have to each other

   ▫ something about how this family live together.

   Example
   My name is Evie and I live with my mum Jenny, her boyfriend Earl and Earl's daughter, Tamika. I share a bedroom with Tamika, we have bunk beds. I see my dad, James every other weekend. My dad lives with my grandma and grandad in a big house. I like going there because my grandad cooks the best Sunday lunch. Sometimes Tamika comes too. She calls my dad James, my grandma Julie, and my grandad Peter. Together, we are all a family.

2. Invite each group to introduce the family they have created, afterwards facilitating a share and compare by asking: How are these families different to each other? How are they similar? Examples could include number of people, siblings and so on, and also positive attributes, such as caring for each other or trust.

Activity 2 (60 minutes)

1. Seat the children around tables, with lolly sticks, card circles, glue and a selection of coloured pens or painting equipment. Explain that everyone is now going to create a family portrait of their own family, to include themselves. Each character will be made from a lolly stick using the larger card circles for the head of an adult and the smaller for the children.

2. Start by drawing the faces on the heads first, using paint or craft materials to make things like hair. Once each head is complete, the children can decorate a lolly stick to represent the person's body, before using craft

materials to make the clothes. Paint pieces of paper or off-cuts of card to make hands and feet, cutting out the shapes once the paint is dry and then sticking in place. Finally, glue the heads onto the dressed lolly stick bodies and leave to dry.

3. Each family member can then be stuck onto a piece of card to create a family portrait. Around the portrait, the children should draw activities they enjoy doing both as a whole family and with individual members, with captions – for example, 'My family likes to go camping' or 'I like making cakes with my dad'. Leave to dry.

4. Display the lolly stick family portraits together to create a Family Wall and to raise awareness about all of the different families the children live in and the hobbies, activities and interests they enjoy. Ask the children to take turns introducing their family portrait to each other. This should include names and the relationship people have to each other, along with things they enjoy doing as a family.

Review (15 minutes)

1. Summarize that a family can be big or small and that families spend time together doing lots of different things. Reinforce that healthy families may look different but have things in common like love, security and safety, which are important in supporting children to grow up safe, confident and emotionally strong.

2. Finally, give each child five sticky labels. On each sticker, the children should write one positive aspect of being in a family, such as love, care. These can be stuck on the Family Wall, around the family portraits as a visual representation of the positive power of families.

LESSON 4: WHAT DOES A POSITIVE FAMILY GIVE US?

Aim

This lesson looks beyond material goods, to the things a healthy family can provide and what makes them important and special.

Learning outcomes

- Be able to define the importance of loyalty and commitment in a family.

- Identify the characteristics that make families healthy, happy and safe.

- Understand how families (and other people who care for us) might help in difficult situations.

Time: 70 minutes

Resources

- Sticky notes and pens

- Copies of the Activity 2: Family Support Worksheet (one copy per group of four to six)

- Activity 3: Diamond 9 Worksheet photocopied onto A3 paper (one per four to six children)

- Large sheets of paper

- Whiteboard and markers

How to do it
Introduction (10 minutes)

1. Start by ensuring that the children all have a common understanding of what a family is and the different shapes and sizes they can be by inviting them to suggest famous families, real or fictional. For example, Harry Potter is famously an orphan, but he is a member of the Dursley family, who are his only living relatives; Darth Vader was revealed to be Luke Sky-walker's father.

Activity 1 (20 minutes)

1. With the children working in groups of four to six, invite them to discuss the following: 'What do our families give us?'

2. Invite a volunteer from each group to make a list of all the ideas on a large sheet of paper.

3. Allow five to ten minutes to discuss and then rotate around the groups inviting a member of each to share something from their list. Record using a simple five-bar gate tally under two headings on the whiteboard; 'Things that Cost Money' (e.g. toys, gifts, devices) and 'Things that Cost Nothing' (e.g. love, kindness, care). At the end, count them up to see which has the most. Acknowledge the list with the most on to the children, making no comment for the moment.

Activity 2 (20 minutes)

1. Now give each group a copy of the Activity 2: Family Support Worksheet and a pen. They should discuss each of the scenarios, imagining what support someone might want or need from their family if that was happening. Allow time for discussions and then invite everyone back together to share and compare their answers.

2. Ask, 'How many of the things you want or need cost money?'

3. Suggest that while presents, gifts and material things can be nice to have, in times of trouble, stress or upset, it is the things that cost nothing but time and emotion that we need and want most from those closest to us.

Activity 3 (15 minutes)

1. Instruct the children to go back to their original list of things families give us. Explain that this time, having discovered the non-material things that families offer, you want them to reflect on the list and choose those they think are most important now.

2. Give each group nine sticky notes, pens and a copy of the Activity 3: Diamond 9 Worksheet. The nine most important things chosen can be written on the sticky notes and then ranked from Most (at the top) to Least (at the bottom) on the worksheet.

3. Invite each group to present their Diamond 9. At the end ask if, after hearing each other's suggestions, any groups want to change or amend the placing of their nine sticky notes. Allow time for this and then display the finalized Diamond 9s under a collective heading, 'Things Our Families Give Us'. Suggest that this helps children to feel secure and cared for, regardless of things that happen outside the family.

Review (5 minutes)

1. Invite each child to suggest one positive thing that a family offers that costs nothing, and how that contributes to family life.

2. Conclude that families should offer a place of safety and security, where people can build mutual relationships based on care, love and trust.

ACTIVITY 2: FAMILY SUPPORT WORKSHEET

Have a look at the situations below. If this happened to you, what support would you like from your family?

Situation 1: When I feel sick or unwell.

. . . .

. . . .

Situation 2: When I feel sad or upset.

. . . .

. . . .

Situation 3: When I hurt myself playing a sport.

. . . .

. . . .

Situation 4: When a friend has been unkind to me.

. . . .

. . . .

Situation 5: When I need help with my homework.

. . . .

. . . .

Situation 6: When I am cold and tired.

. . . .

. . . .

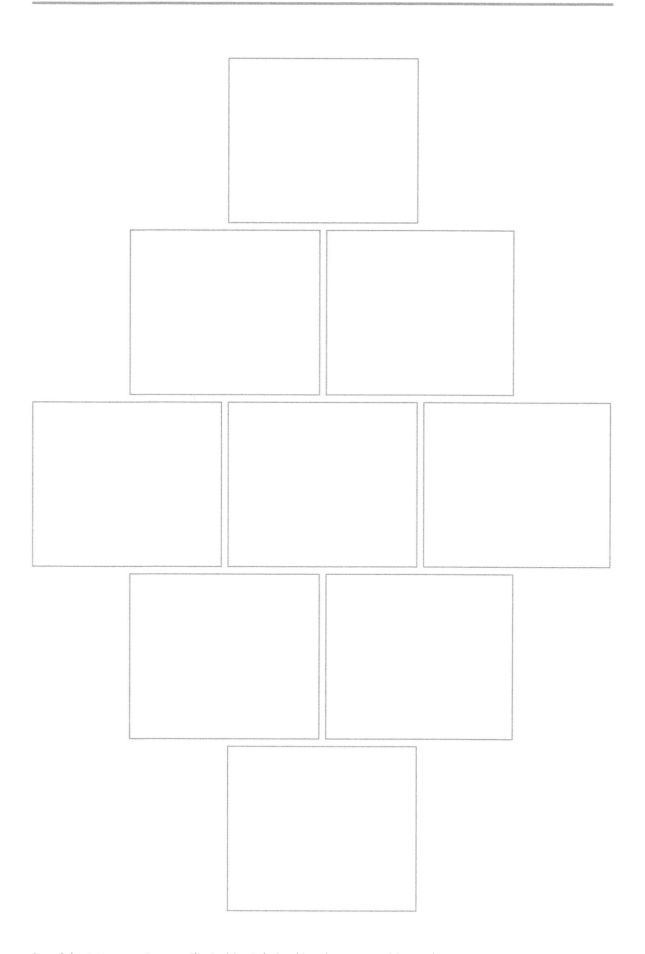

LESSON 5: RECIPROCITY IN FAMILY RELATIONSHIPS

Aim

To explore the concept of reciprocity in families and develop skills for building healthy and supportive relationships.

Learning outcomes

- Understand that positive, healthy family relationships require give and take.

- Recognize that by helping others you can help yourself develop new skills, increase confidence and a sense of pride.

Time: 80 minutes

Resources

- Sets of the Activity 1: Roles and Responsibilities Cards (one per group of six children)

- Sets of the Activity 2: Reciprocal Acts of Kindness Cards

- Copies of the Activity 3: Daily Acts of Kindness Worksheet and pens

How to do it
Introduction (5 minutes)

1. Ask the children if they have heard the term 'give and take' and if so, what they think it means. Discuss ideas and then suggest that a word to describe give and take is 'reciprocity', which refers to the mutual exchange of actions, feelings or support between individuals in a relationship. Reciprocity contributes to building strong and harmonious families where everyone feels respected and valued. For example, if one family member cooks a meal and someone else washes up, there has been a reciprocal exchange of actions.

Activity 1 (20 minutes)

1. Divide the class into small groups, giving out large sheets of paper, pens and a set of Activity 1: Roles and Responsibilities Cards. Ask for a volunteer from each group to draw a large picture of a house in the middle of a sheet of paper. Inside the house, write down all the family members with whom the children live, or who spend a lot of time at their home, such as parents/carers, siblings, grandparents. This will look slightly different for each group.

2. Next, ask the children to consider what each family member depicted in the group 'house' contributes to family life by matching them with the responsibilities on the Activity 1: Roles and Responsibilities Cards. If the children identify extra family responsibilities, they can add these too.

3. Facilitate a class discussion, allowing each group to share their findings and explore the concept of reciprocity in fulfilling these roles. Ask questions about the different roles people are taking in the home; for example, who does most of the cooking, helps with homework, looks after pets. Invite the children to tell each other about any family 'jobs' they have, like washing up or making their bed.

4. Using their pictures as a discussion point, ask the young people to suggest other things family members do for each other, which may not have a monetary value, such as love, care and emotional support. Point out that this will differ between families.

Activity 2 (25 minutes)

1. Ask the children to work in pairs, and hand each couple one of the family situations on the Activity 2: Reciprocal Acts of Kindness Cards. Their task is to devise a role-play to show what is happening in the scenario and the reciprocal actions that could be taken.

2. Invite the pairs to take turns in acting out their new scenario, demonstrating how reciprocity can be practised with different family members, and their response.

3. After each role-play, encourage the rest of the class to review what they saw. How might this type of reciprocal act strengthen family relationships?

Activity 3 (20 minutes)

1. Give each child an Activity 3: Daily Acts of Kindness Worksheet and a pen. Explain that this is to help them reflect individually on their daily interactions with family members and then pledge a new reciprocal act of kindness in the left-hand column. Remind them that this can be an action,

feeling or type of support and has nothing to do with how much money is given or spent.

2. Discuss the impact of these acts on their family relationships and how reciprocity contributes to a positive family dynamic. Finally, challenge the children to perform these acts of kindness for their family members over a designated period (e.g. a week), recording in the right-hand column of the worksheet their actions and what happened.

3. These can be reviewed back in the classroom in pairs at a later date.

Review (10 minutes)

1. Recap the main points about reciprocity in families, emphasizing the need for building balance and fairness. Encourage the children to practise their acts of kindness with different family members and encourage them to appreciate the things that are done for them.

2. Conclude that in healthy, positive families everyone takes some responsibility for family tasks and nurturing the relationships, so everyone feels valued and appreciated.

ACTIVITY 1: ROLES AND RESPONSIBILITIES CARDS

Housework	**Cooking**	**Helping with homework**
Washing up	**Drying up**	**Laundry**
Food shopping	**Babysitting**	**Taking children to and from school**

Gardening	Clothes shopping	Mending things
Childcare	Looking after pets	Going to work
Reading bedtime stories	Playing games	Making packed lunches

Ironing	Organizing family events	Taking rubbish out
Making the beds	Washing windows	Painting and decorating

Your older sibling stops watching their favourite TV show to help you with your homework.

What reciprocal act of kindness could you do?

Your parent cooks you a vegan meal as well as the meat dish that everyone else in the family prefers to eat.

What reciprocal act of kindness could you do?

Your cousin walks all the way to your house to bring you a jumper you left behind in case you need it.

What reciprocal act of kindness could you do?

Your grandparent stops working to give you good advice on how to tackle a difficult challenge.

What reciprocal act of kindness could you do?

Your sibling lends you their favourite top to wear to a party.

What reciprocal act of kindness could you do?

Instead of going out, your parent spends hours listening to you practising your lines for the school play.

What reciprocal act of kindness could you do?

Your grandparent comes round to look after you while you are off school sick.

What reciprocal act of kindness could you do?

Your older sibling takes you out to the park in the rain to practise football as you have a match tomorrow.

What reciprocal act of kindness could you do?

Your parent helps you learn a new skill, like riding a bike or skateboarding.

What reciprocal act of kindness could you do?

Your younger sibling feeds your pet while you are away on a school trip.

What reciprocal act of kindness could you do?

ACTIVITY 3: DAILY ACTS OF KINDNESS WORKSHEET

My daily act of kindness	What happened
When: Who: What:	
When: Who: What:	
When: Who: What:	
When: Who: What:	
When: Who: What:	
When: Who: What:	
When: Who: What:	
When: Who: What:	

LESSON 6: FAMILY CELEBRATIONS

Aim

Based on a well-known game, this lesson enables children to share and compare the things they like to do and celebrate as a family.

Learning outcomes

- Understand that people have a wide range of ways to enjoy family time but central to that is to feel safe and cared for.

- Recognize different faith, cultural and social events that families celebrate, and ways they are celebrated.

- Come up with suggestions for new activities, games and so on to take home and share.

Time: 45 minutes

Resources

- Copies of the Activity 1: Family Bingo Sheet (one per child)

- Art supplies (coloured pencils, felt tip and marker pens)

- Handwriting pens

How to do it
Introduction (10 minutes)

1. Write the word FAMILY vertically down one side of a whiteboard. Working through each of the letters in turn, invite the class to call out positive words related to family. Using different coloured pens, write the suggestions beside each letter across the whiteboard. For example, 'F': fairness, food, friendship, fun, faith.

2. When all of the ideas have been exhausted, conclude that while all families are slightly different, healthy positive families are characterized by love and care.

Activity 1 (30 minutes)

1. Give each child an Activity 1: Family Bingo Sheet and access to a wide selection of coloured pens. On it, they should write their name and then decorate the area around the grid (leaving the squares blank) to represent their family.

2. Next, call out the following questions, inviting each child to write their answer into the corresponding square on the grid before moving to the next one. Alternatively, you could ask children to draw their answer in the square.
   Family Bingo questions:

   ▨ Square 1: Something you enjoy doing with your family at the weekend.

   ▨ Square 2: A family movie/TV show you like watching together.

   ▨ Square 3: A faith or cultural event you celebrate as a family.

   ▨ Square 4: A favourite meal your family eats together.

   ▨ Square 5: Something you do together outside the home.

   ▨ Square 6: How birthdays are celebrated in your family.

   ▨ Square 7: A game you like playing with one or more family members.

   ▨ Square 8: A song or music that reminds you of home.

   ▨ Square 9: One thing that makes your family special.

3. Once the sheets are complete, it is time to play Family Bingo. Ask everyone to stand up in a clear area where they can freely move about the room.

4. Read out the questions again, this time allowing time in between for the children to walk around and talk to each other to share and compare answers until they find one that matches their own. For example, if one child has written that their family's favourite meal is a roast dinner, they need to find another child who has also written a roast in square four. Once matched, the other child can write their name in the appropriate square on the Family Bingo sheet. Encourage the children to talk together as much as possible rather than sticking to their friendship groups, so they get to learn more about their peers.

5. Keep going until someone matches all nine squares, when they should loudly call out 'Family Bingo!' Lead a round of applause to congratulate their achievement and then continue until everyone has completed the task.

Activity 2 (10 minutes)

1. With the children in pairs, invite them to share in more detail how they celebrate family events, different traditions and faith holidays to raise awareness and learn from the diversity within the group. Each couple should identify one thing that is similar and one thing that is different about their family to share later.

2. Bring everyone back together in a seated circle and invite each couple to share their findings, encouraging other children to contribute with their own similarities or difference afterwards. Conclude that while many families celebrate things like birthdays, Diwali and Christmas, most families have their own traditions too, such as family recipes handed down through the generations, or family stories about where they live and their journey there.

Review (10 minutes)

1. Recap on the experience of learning how families celebrate in different ways. Suggest that while family life might be different, celebrating traditions and spending time together doing things they enjoy strengthens relationships and builds bonds that can last for life. Finally, display the Family Bingo sheets as a reminder that each family is special and unique.

Extension activity

Set children the challenge of interviewing an older family member about one of the customs, celebrations or traditions identified to find out how it was celebrated when they were a child. This can be shared later with their peers and the information added to the Family Bingo display.

ACTIVITY 1: FAMILY BINGO SHEET

Name: . . . .

1.	**2.**	**3.**
4.	**5.**	**6.**
7.	**8.**	**9.**

CHAPTER 3

Caring Friendships

KEY WORDS

Healthy friendships, trust, consent, kindness, respect, mutual support, loyalty and inclusion, boundaries and conflict

LESSON 1: IDENTIFYING THE KEY CHARACTERISTICS OF FRIENDSHIP

Aim

The activities in this lesson identify the characteristics of friendship and the personal skills and qualities that make someone a good friend to others.

Learning outcomes

- Recognize that everyone is unique but there are core characteristics that make a friendship healthy and positive.

- Identify the personal qualities and skills each child can offer a potential friend.

Time: 60 minutes

Resources

- Copies of the Activity 1: Friendship Gold Worksheet (enlarged to A3)

- Coloured drawing pens/pencils

- Whiteboard and markers

- A sheet of A4 stiff paper (one per child)

- Art supplies (pencils, coloured pens etc.)

- Glue and wooden lolly sticks

Top tip: These activities work best with established groups or classes where the children know each other well.

How to do it
Introduction (15 minutes)

1. Seat everyone in a circle. This is a word-association game, where each child in turn suggests a word related to 'friendship'. This could include alternative names for a 'friend', such as buddy, mate, bestie, or positive attributes linked to friendship, such as trust, respect, fun. If someone can't think of a word they must shout 'Word Gap!' and wait until the next

round to try again. After two 'Word Gap' turns, they are out. The last child to contribute a friendship word wins the game and is congratulated with a round of applause.

Activity 1 (20 minutes)

1. Divide the children into small groups of four or five. Give each group an Activity 1: Friendship Gold Worksheet and a selection of coloured pens. Explain that the treasure chest on the worksheet is filled with gold coins and each coin represents a skill, quality or characteristic important in a good friendship. Task each group with discussing and agreeing the six friendship characteristics they think most valuable and then designing their own gold coins to add to the chest. The coins can be any shape or size, but the design for each one must include the name of a chosen characteristic.

2. Bring the whole group together to share and compare the characteristics they think most valuable and why. Record these on a whiteboard to include:

   - mutual respect

   - honesty

   - trustworthiness

   - loyalty

   - support.

3. Conclude that all friendships are different and unique, but there are common characteristics that make them positive and healthy.

Activity 2 (15 minutes)

1. Back in their small groups, give each child a pen and a sheet of stiff paper. They are each going to make a simple fan.

2. Begin by instructing the children to decorate one side of their paper with their name and symbols, signs or motifs.

3. Then, starting at one end of the paper, instruct everyone to fold about 2.5cm of paper down. Turn the paper over and fold another 2.5cm down and repeat until the entire paper has been folded, concertina style. Press down hard along the folded paper to keep the fan in place and then fold the entire fan in half.

4. Turn the fan over so that the blank side of the fan is face up. Each child should write their name in large letters on the first blank space under the first fold of the fan then pass the fan to the person on their left to write a friendship skill or quality they think the owner of the fan possesses

on the second blank space. Repeat this process until all the folds on the undecorated side of the fan have been filled with positive comments apart from the middle one on each side, which needs to stay blank. Then return the fan to its owner.

5. Every child in the class now has a 'fan' full of positive attributes that combine to make them a good friend to someone else. Invite them to spend a few minutes reviewing what has been written and then facilitate reflection by using the following prompt questions:

   ▪ Do you agree with the reasons why your peers say you make (or would make) a good friend?

   ▪ What do you consider your strongest friendship quality?

   ▪ Are these the same things you look for in a friendship?

6. To complete the fan, instruct the children to pull the top edges of both sides of the fan together, and then glue them in place. Hold until dry to stop the fan springing apart and then make a handle by gluing a lolly stick over the middle seam at the bottom, leaving enough free to hold it by.

Review (10 minutes)

1. Facilitate a circle time activity, inviting each child to say one thing they value in a friend, followed by one thing they believe they contribute to a positive friendship.

2. Conclude that while all friendships are slightly different, core positive characteristics like trust, respect and kindness help to make it last.

ACTIVITY 1: FRIENDSHIP GOLD WORKSHEET

LESSON 2: THE IMPORTANCE OF FRIENDSHIP

Aim

This lesson encourages children to think about the importance of friendship and the positive qualities to look for in a friend.

Learning outcomes

- Understand the importance of friendship and the positive value it adds to our lives.

- Recognize the key features that make a healthy friendship.

- Understand that healthy friendship is a two-way process, where each person gives and receives.

Time: 60 minutes

Resources

- Copies of the Activity 2: Friend Word Bank

- Large sheets of poster paper

- Art supplies (coloured pencils, felt tip and marker pens)

How to do it
Introduction (10 minutes)

1. In a seated circle, invite each child to complete the sentence, 'A friend is someone who...'

2. Repeat another round, this time asking the children to suggest one thing a friend is not.

3. Conclude with a final round that asks each child to nominate someone and then share one personal characteristic that they think makes them a good friend. For example, 'Anna for being a good listener.'

Activity 1 (20 minutes)

1. This is a feet-first activity to spark discussion and encourage critical thinking about the importance of friendships to wellbeing. Ask the children to listen to the following statements and choice of answers and then move to one point in the room if they agree, another if they disagree and to stand somewhere in the middle if they are not sure or need more information to form an opinion.
Statements (the correct answers are in *italic*):

Having strong friendships positively impacts on your overall wellbeing.

- *Agree: Friends provide emotional support, companionship, and a sense of identity and belonging, which can all contribute to overall wellbeing.*

- Disagree: Friends do not impact on your wellbeing; you don't need friends to feel good.

You can have too many friends, which is bad for your emotional wellbeing.

- Agree: No one needs more than a few friends, any more take too much effort.

- *Disagree: As long as the friendships are healthy, there is no such thing as too many friends.*

Having no friends can trigger loneliness, which negatively affects your mental and physical health.

- *Agree: Social isolation can lead to loneliness, which increases the risk of mental health issues such as depression and anxiety, as well as physical health problems.*

- Disagree: Loneliness and lack of social connections has nothing to do with your mental and physical health.

Friends provide a support system that can help you cope better in difficult times.

- *Agree: Friends can offer a listening ear, emotional support, advice and encouragement during difficult times, which can all help you.*

- Disagree: Friends have no impact on the ability to cope with challenges. You have to sort out your own problems.

2. Encourage discussion between each round, exploring why children think their friendships are important to them and finding examples of how they have supported friends in difficult times. Conclude that good friends can increase happiness levels and contribute to overall happiness and life satisfaction.

Activity 2 (20 minutes)

1. Divide the class into small groups, each with an Activity 2: Friend Word Bank worksheet and a pen. Explain that the first task is to identify the key features they think essential in a good friend. This could be based on a real person or a mixture of the things they like about different people. Once identified, the top six attributes can be written in the box on the worksheet.

2. Next, give out large sheets of paper and art supplies. Task each group with creating a poster (or meme) to celebrate the importance of friendship. This can be in any style, and can be a combination of words and pictures, but must include the words they have selected from the Friend Word Bank.

3. Invite the children to share and compare posters to see the things most popularly selected as important, making it clear that there may well be differences in opinions as we all value different things in our friendships.

4. The posters can be displayed together to remind everyone of the skills and qualities of friendship and the importance of friends.

Review (10 minutes)

1. Ask the children to pick up their completed worksheets and bring them back into a seated circle. Explain that each child is going to select in turn from the word bank something positive that they believe they *bring* to a friendship – the things that potentially make them a good friend to others.

2. Facilitate a short conversation about the importance of reciprocity within friendships, for example if you value loyalty and kindness in others, you should be prepared to offer it back.

3. Conclude by making the point that being a good friend is about who you are on the inside, the real you, rather than what someone looks like or who is cool to hang out with. While we might all like different people, or have friends with whom we do different activities, the core qualities identified here like trust, mutual respect, and honesty, are the things more likely to make a healthy friendship last.

ACTIVITY 2: FRIEND WORD BANK

Have a look at the word bank below:

Generous	Daring	Honest	Quiet	Trustworthy
Thoughtful	Important	Non-judgemental	Attentive	Demanding
Selfish	Affectionate	Funny	Aggressive	Spirited
Open-minded	Clever	Special	Emotional	Talkative
Committed	Dynamic	Assertive	Determined	Decisive
Understanding	Friendly	Supportive	Helpful	Amazing
Open	Kind	Encouraging	Respectful	Good looking
Talented	Quick witted	Careful	Competitive	Reliable
Cool	Fast	Unpredictable	Slow	Opinionated
Resourceful	Loyal	Strong	Caring	Resilient

Which six characteristics are most important to you in a friend?

1		4	
2		5	
3		6	

LESSON 3: FRIENDSHIP AND BOUNDARIES

Aim

To explore the notion of friends, boundaries in a healthy friendship and how far loyalty should extend.

Learning outcomes

- Understand that there are boundaries set in a healthy friendship.

- Identify ways to maintain personal boundaries and remain friends.

- Recognize the difference between loyalty and peer pressure.

Time: 60 minutes

Resources

- Copies of the Activity 2: Things a Friend Should Do Worksheet (one for each child)

- Pens/pencils

How to do it
Introduction (10 minutes)

1. Ask the children to stand in a circle, facing inwards and holding hands with the person on either side of them. Now ask everyone to take a step towards the middle, still holding hands.

2. Repeat until they are all close together and then explain that they are going to get closer and closer until they come to the edge of each other's personal space. Define personal space as the gap we like between us and another, which can be different for each person. Suggest that they will know if someone is too close because it is the point when they start feeling crowded or uncomfortable, even if they know the other person well and/or like them.

3. At this point, tell the children to shout 'Stop!', and everyone must stay where they are. Review the different amount of space people need around them,

asking how it felt as their personal boundary was reached, stressing that any form of touch requires consent.

Activity 2 (20 minutes)

1. This game continues to explore healthy friendships, respect and boundaries. It can be done as a whole class challenge or you can divide the children into teams and play it as a competition.

2. Tell each child to reach out their left hand and grab the hand of someone across the circle from them. Next, instruct them to reach out their right hand and grab the hand of a different person across the circle. This will create a 'human knot'.

3. Challenge the children to work together to untangle the knot and return to the standing circle without letting go of each other's hands. While being mindful of personal space, they can negotiate with each other to step over or under arms, twist and turn, all the while communicating with each other to find a solution. The only rule is that they must obtain consent from those holding their hands before each move.

4. Once everyone has successfully untangled themselves and formed a circle again, review the activity discussing how they managed to solve the human knot, how they managed to respect personal boundaries and the importance of communication, teamwork, and supporting one another.

Activity 2 (20 minutes)

1. Next, give each child a pen and a copy of the Activity 2: Things a Friend Should Do Worksheet to complete, privately at this stage. Go through the worksheet, sharing and comparing answers and discussing issues raised. Facilitate a discussion that considers the following:

   ▨ In friendship, is there any room for different interests, tastes and opinions?

   ▨ Should best friends be exclusive, or is it healthy to have other friends?

   ▨ Should a friend always keep a secret? When might a confidence have to be broken?

2. Take the opportunity to talk about confidentiality and that being a true friend may mean breaking a secret to tell a trusted adult if someone tells you something that is harmful or potentially dangerous.

Review (10 minutes)

1. Conclude that friendships are fun and should offer mutual care and support. However, it is important to respect each person's emotional and physical boundaries to maintain a healthy, balanced friendship that benefits both people. If not, suggest the friendship is likely to become unhappy, leading to conflict and potentially one or both people not wanting to be friends anymore. Similarly, it is healthy to develop a circle of friends and acquaintances, rather than relying solely on one person or becoming jealous and possessive if they have other friends.

ACTIVITY 2: THINGS A FRIEND SHOULD DO WORKSHEET

Friends should:	True	Maybe	False
Listen to each other			
Help each other			
Find each other funny			
Be honest with each other			
Feel upset if they have other friends			
Always agree with each other			
Be equally good at the same things			
Be mindful of each other's feelings			
Share everything they have			
Talk about hopes and dreams			
Never argue			
Stick up for each other			
Keep each other's secrets			
Share in each other's happiness			
Give each other gifts			

LESSON 4: FRIENDSHIP DILEMMAS

Aim

The cards in this activity enable children to discuss the meaning of friendship and how to be a good friend in a range of scenarios.

Learning outcomes

- Understand the importance of empathy, support and kindness within friendships.

- Identify positive and negative emotions triggered in a range of friendship scenarios, and how to cope with them.

- Know when to get advice or support from a trusted adult.

Time: 60 minutes

Resources

- Copies of the Activity 1: Friendship Dilemmas (photocopied, enlarged and cut up ready to play)

- Two A3 sheets of paper and a marker pen

- Paper and pens

How to do it
Introduction (10 minutes)

1. Gather the children in a seated circle and set the scene with a quick discussion about friendship. Ask questions such as:

   - What does friendship mean to you?

   - How does having friends make you feel?

Activity 1 (30 minutes)

1. To prepare, take the two sheets of A3 paper and write in large letters the words 'Good Friend' on one and 'Not a Friend' on the other. Place them equal distance apart on the floor to create a Friendship Continuum.

2. Give each child one of the Activity 1: Friendship Dilemmas, face down so they cannot see it. Explain that you are going to invite each child in turn to read out their scenario and then place it where they think it should go on the Friendship Continuum. The nearer the 'Good Friend' end, the more they think that the child in the scenario has shown one or more of the characteristics of friendship, for example been kind, thoughtful or caring, compared to the opposite pole, 'Not a Friend', where someone has done nothing friendly at all.

3. For each scenario, ask the child to explain where they place it and why. Once this has been done, invite comments from the other children. Do they agree with the placement? If not, why not.

4. Once all of the cards have been laid on the continuum, choose some from both ends to discuss further using these prompt questions:

   ▢ How might both children in the scenario be feeling?

   ▢ What could be done to resolve any tensions or disagreements?

   ▢ Who could the children go to for help and support (e.g. a parent/carer, teacher)?

5. Reiterate the foundations of a healthy friendship to include trust, mutual respect, kindness, thoughtfulness and empathy (i.e. the ability to understand how someone else might be feeling).

Activity 2 (10 minutes)

1. With the children working in pairs, ask them to consider their current friendships. Do they meet the requirements discussed for a good friend and a healthy friendship? If not, why not. Suggest that some things are within our control, for example if you have a friend who you don't see very often you could find different ways to keep in touch, perhaps by phone, text or social media. However, some things are outside our control, for example someone being mean, or who upsets you.

2. Together, task each couple with coming up with one example of a way they could strengthen a friendship and someone they could tell or go to for help if there are difficulties in a friendship that they cannot resolve on their own.

Review (10 minutes)

1. Invite each pair to share their examples, reinforcing positive ideas and suggestions for strengthening friendships while making it clear that if

anyone feels pressured into doing something they don't want to, or that is dangerous, potentially harmful or wrong, it is best to go to a trusted adult for support and guidance. Make sure that every child has identified someone they can ask for help before closing.

ACTIVITY 1: FRIENDSHIP DILEMMAS

Sophie feels unwell. Dara offers to sit quietly with her during playtime.

Yasmin wants to play basketball. Angus tells her to go play netball with the other girls.

Tulip tells Remi something private. Remi tells the whole class.

Jonas wants to play with Charlie, but he says he is already playing with Amy.

Kemi borrows Ali's pen and breaks it. He decides to keep quiet and say nothing.

Billy loves football. Tilly wants to be Billy's friend so pretends to like it too.

Ashraf secretly takes a photo of Tommy and refuses to delete it when asked.

Viktorija has a mobile phone. When she makes a call, Candy pushes her, so she drops it.

Jay borrows Sam's ruler without asking. Jay says she won't mind.

Tai hides Lo's school bag for a joke. The more upset Lo gets, the more Tai laughs.

Sandy is crying. Giacomo tells her to stop being silly.

Lola accepts May's invite to tea then pretends to be sick so she can go out with Daisy.

Joe sees older children teasing Dan. He is scared to challenge so asks an adult for help.

Sarah is asked about her family. Josh sees her getting upset so asks if she'd like to play.

Lucy is new in class. Henry invites her to sit next to him.

Lilly tells Maya to stop being nasty to Sean. Maya tells her to mind her own business.

Sunni overhears children gossiping about his friend, so he yells at them to 'shut up'.

Elijah and Abe are sharing a pizza. One piece is much bigger, so Elijah offers it to Abe.

Skye is told to share her sweets. Instead she hides them to eat later alone.

Reggie kicks a football that hits Ruby's head. He refuses to apologize because it was an accident.

LESSON 5: CHALLENGES AND MAINTAINING FRIENDSHIPS

Aim

This lesson explores potential challenges and conflicts within a friendship and ways to maintain it so that it can continue in a healthy way.

Learning outcomes

- Understand that people have different needs and expectations from friendships.

- Find positive ways to manage disagreements within a friendship.

- Identify possible reasons why a friendship should not be maintained, and how to end it.

Time: 70 minutes

Resources

- Paper slips and a box

- Handwriting pens

- Large sheets of paper

- Glue sticks

- Art supplies (coloured pencils, felt tip and marker pens)

- Activity 3: Role-Play Cards

How to do it
Introduction (15 minutes)

1. Open the topic by playing a 'feet first' game to explore attitudes to friends and friendship groups. Assign different points in the room, 'Just like me', 'A bit like me' and 'Nothing like me'. Explain that you are going to read out a series of statements after which each child should go to the point in the room that best reflects their opinion.

Statements

- I have lots of different friends related to all my interests and hobbies.

- I have one close friend, who I do everything with.

- I prefer my own company and like things I can do alone.

- Most of my friends are online, which is where we meet and socialize.

- I have a group of friends in school and others I know from home.

- My best friends are my family.

2. Take time between statements to explore feelings and attitudes to friendship, especially where different views are expressed. Conclude that while everyone has different friendship needs, keeping a healthy friendship going requires things like empathy, respect, mutual support, loyalty and kindness.

Activity 1 (20 minutes)

1. Invite everyone to choose a partner to work with then ask them to discuss: 'What might cause a friendship to change?'

2. Give out the slips of paper and pens so they can write their key suggestions down. Ideas for changing friendships could include:

- someone moving away

- arguments

- moving into a different interest based peer group

- transition to secondary school.

Note: older children may suggest changes that a romantic relationship can have on existing friendships, so be ready to respond if that happens. Make sure they understand the importance of maintaining existing friendships and other support networks, rather than becoming isolated and dependent on the new relationship alone.

3. Collect the slips of paper into a box and then shake to shuffle. Read these out and cluster into similar themes to prevent duplication, then divide the children into small groups, giving each a maximum of three different ideas to consider in more detail.

4. Allocate large sheets of paper, pens, and a glue stick. Ask a volunteer from each group to write the title, 'Friendship Dilemma 1' at the top of the first sheet and then using the glue, stick the first slip of paper underneath it. The group task is to discuss potential difficulties that could arise in a friendship in the situation outlined on the paper, before considering things

that could be done to maintain, nurture and strengthen the friendship, if appropriate. Key points can be recorded using bullet points under the sub-headings, 'Challenges to the Friendship' and 'Ways to Maintain the Friendship'.

Example: Friendship dilemma: moving home
Challenges to the friendship:

◙ Not having daily contact.

◙ Fewer shared experiences.

◙ New school/activities.

Ways to maintain the friendship:

◙ Keeping in touch via text, phone or social media.

◙ Asking questions about your friend's new home.

◙ Keeping up shared interests.

This process can be repeated to explore each of the friendship dilemmas, using a newly numbered piece of paper each time.

5. Allow time to complete the task and then invite each group to present their first scenario, why they think the situation has put the friendship under pressure and ways a healthy friendship could be maintained. If things like negotiation, compromise and apologies have not been suggested, introduce them.

Activity 2 (10 minutes)

1. Facilitate a whole group discussion that asks: 'Is there ever a time when a friendship should not be maintained?'

2. In addition to things like growing apart or finding new friends, suggestions could include when a friendship is no longer healthy, for example when there is peer pressure, bullying, or other unacceptable behaviour. Explain that while there are likely to be disagreements within a friendship, if it is a positive, healthy relationship there should be room to discuss different points of view to reach a compromise or accept and respect a difference of opinion. The exception to this is where someone is at risk of being harmed or harming others, in which case adult help should be sought.

Activity 3 (20 minutes)

1. With the children working in threes, use the Activity 3: Role-Play Cards to explore the different scenarios. While two children assume the characters

of the 'friends', the third will silently watch proceedings and then offer feedback on how well the challenging situation was resolved.

2. Rotate roles using the three different scenarios until each child has experienced being a participant on both sides of the challenge, plus been an observer and offered feedback.

3. Bring the whole class back together, inviting comments on what they saw and experienced in terms of what worked and what was not so effective.

4. Summarize by reminding the children that in healthy, positive relationships differences are resolved by:

   ▪ valuing diversity

   ▪ talking and respecting different opinions

   ▪ actively listening to each other

   ▪ working towards a compromise, where appropriate

   ▪ assertively (not aggressively) saying what you think, want or need

   ▪ apologizing when you are wrong

   ▪ resisting peer pressure – friends do not force each other to do things they don't want to do or know to be wrong.

Review (5 minutes)

1. Recap on the main points discussed in the lesson, particularly that in any friendship there are likely to be ups and downs. Summarize that all friendships require maintenance to flourish and grow, particularly when under pressure from external influences. While some of these can be anticipated and planned for, others are likely to require things like patience, tolerance, respect and kindness from everyone involved. However, if a friendship is making you feel anxious, unhappy or scared, it is time to ask for help from a trusted adult.

ACTIVITY 3: ROLE-PLAY CARDS

Role-play one

Jamie lent Susie his favourite pen and when he asks for it back, she tells him it's lost. When Jamie gets upset, she says that it is his fault for lending it to her.

Jamie is furious, she has disrespected his property. Susie can't see what all the fuss is about, it is only a pen, and he has lots of them.

Role-play two

Friends Sami and Jed both want pizza for school lunch but there is only one portion left. Sami sticks his finger in the pizza – now he will have to have it. Jed is furious, how dare Sami touch food that doesn't belong to him? It shows how selfish he is.

They argue and when Jed shoves Sami, the pizza falls off the plate onto the floor.

Role-play three

Bronte and Taylor are best friends and usually do everything together. Yesterday the teacher sat Taylor with someone else and she really enjoyed it. Usually, Bronte makes all the decisions and sulks if he can't get his own way, so it was nice to do what she wanted for a change.

Taylor decides she has to say something if their friendship is to continue.

LESSON 6: CHANGING FRIENDSHIPS

Aim

This activity explores how and why friendships and friendship groups can change during times of transition, particularly moving from primary to secondary school.

Learning outcomes

- Identify some of the potential pressures on friendships during times of transition.

- Recognize feelings and emotions associated with friendships during times of transition.

- Understand the benefits and challenges of developing new friendships, while maintaining existing ones.

Time: 60 minutes

Resources

- A ball

- Copies of the Activity 1: Changing Friends Scenarios

- Paper and pens

How to do it
Introduction (10 minutes)

1. Ask the class to stand in a circle. Start the exercise standing in the middle, holding a ball. Complete the sentence, 'My friends are important to me because...' then throw the ball to one of the children who repeats the sentence, adding their own ideas and throws it to someone else who in turn completes the sentence and passes the ball on.

2. Facilitate a second round, this time asking each child to complete the sentence 'A good way to make a new friend is...' Ideas could include:

   - smiling

   - a friendship request on social media (check it is age-appropriate first)

- inviting someone to join a game

- introducing yourself

- asking someone a few questions about themselves

- sharing food.

Activity 1 (20 minutes)

1. With the children in pairs, invite them to share their experiences of making new friends. This could be a short-term friendship, like those made on holiday, or the story of how they met their best friend.

2. Explain that while some people only have one or two life-long friends, many develop new friendships throughout their life, for example when they transition to secondary school, start a new job or move house.

3. Seat the children in small groups, each with one of the Activity 1: Changing Friends Scenarios, pens and blank paper. Explain that in each scenario a child is getting ready to leave primary school and start secondary school after the summer holidays. The task for each group is to help the child overcome their friendship anxieties, so that they feel confident and ready to move on. Once they have discussed the questions, they should write a letter to the character in their scenario offering advice, support and guidance on how to make things better.

4. Invite each group to present their scenario and letter, inviting any extra suggestions from the rest of the class after each one.

5. Summarize that while it can be a challenge to move to a new school, maintaining existing friendships, agreeing ways to keep in touch with those you will no longer see every day and preparing mentally and physically to be proactive in making new ones can all help build confidence and coping skills.

Activity 2 (20 minutes)

1. Explain to the children that they will be creating a friendship circle, which will be a visual representation of the importance of friendship.

2. Provide each child with a large sheet of paper, a pencil and a selection of coloured pens. Demonstrate by placing your left foot on the paper and lightly tracing around it in pencil, then instruct the children to do the same. Once finished, each child can decorate their foot using colours, patterns and symbols to represent their personality and what makes them a good friend. Tell them to take care not to go over the edge as only the footprint will be used.

3. Once they have finished decorating their feet, pass round scissors and ask the children to cut them out. The left-over paper can be recycled.

4. Clear space on the floor or a wall and draw a large circle using a simple compass made of string attached to chalk at one end and a drawing pin (or similar) at the other. Anchor the drawing pin to the floor; the length of string will create the radius of the circle. Pulling the string to its full length, use the chalk to draw a circle. If the string stays taught, the circle should come out perfectly. Once done, remove the compass.

5. Invite each child in turn to come up to the circle to place their decorated foot on the chalk circle, arranging them so they overlap and connect with each other. When complete, explain that this friendship circle represents the power of friends and the strength of having good friends.

6. Ask the children to reflect on their work using these prompt questions:

   ▫ How do you feel seeing all the feet connected?

   ▫ What does this activity teach us about the importance of friendship?

   ▫ How can we be good friends to others?

Review (10 minutes)

1. Instruct the children to form a circle around the Friendship Circle. Ask each child to share one thing they will do to be a good friend to others, now and in the future (e.g. now – listening to friends' anxieties about moving school; in the future – making the effort to say hello to new classmates rather than waiting for them to do it).

Extension activity

Set the children the task of designing a meme or hashtag to be used as part of a campaign to promote the benefits of new friendships.

ACTIVITY 1: CHANGING FRIENDS SCENARIOS

Scenario 1

Milly is going into Year 7 in September. Romy is the only other child from Milly's primary school to be going to the same secondary school. Currently Milly and Romy are not really friends as they are in different classes and go to different after-school clubs.

- How is Milly feeling?
- What is she concerned about?
- What could be done to make things better?

Scenario 2

Johnnie is the top goal scorer for his primary school football team and is looking forward to playing in secondary school. His friend Fred tells him not to boast as he might not make the new school team, and they end up arguing.

- How is Johnnie feeling?
- What is he concerned about?
- What could be done to make things better?

Scenario 3

Tai and Betty have been best friends since nursery. Betty keeps saying how much she is looking forward to making new friends when they start secondary school. Tai doesn't feel the same. He is happy to keep Betty as his best friend and doesn't want new friends.

- How is Tai feeling?
- What is he concerned about?
- What could be done to make things better?

Scenario 4

Lola has just moved to a new house and changed schools. She doesn't know anyone locally but has seen a girl about her age living next door. The girl is wearing the same uniform as Lola's new school, so she wonders if they could become friends.

- How is Lola feeling?
- What is she concerned about?
- What could be done to make things better?

CHAPTER 4

Respectful Relationships

KEY WORDS

Friendship, relationship, communication, peer pressure, consent, boundaries, conflict, negotiation, apology, compromise and stereotypes

LESSON 1: THE IMPORTANCE OF LISTENING

Aim

This lesson explores the importance of listening and hearing within a healthy friendship. It introduces the idea of selective listening – only hearing the parts of a message that seem relevant while ignoring the rest – and the potential consequences of miscommunication.

Learning outcomes

- Understand the importance of effective communication in a friendship.

- Know the meaning of selective listening and how it can lead to arguments.

- Identify how to actively listen.

Time: 50 minutes

Resources

- A paragraph from a storybook

- A4 paper

- Art supplies (coloured pencils, felt tip and marker pens)

How to do it
Introduction (10 minutes)

1. Demonstrate the importance of listening and mutual responsibility in communication by reading out the same paragraph from a story of your choice, twice. The topic is not important but it should include descriptions and character dialogue.

2. The first time you read it aloud, do so in a dull, monotone voice, making sure there is no attempt to give the characters different voices or to differentiate between action and description. Then swiftly re-read it, this time in a lively way that is as engaging as possible to bring the characters to life.

3. Ask the children, in pairs, to reflect on both readings. Which was easiest to listen to, and why? Which one had the most meaning?

4. Invite feedback, encouraging conversation about their experiences. Suggest that communication is a two-way process, with both the speaker and the listener playing an active role to find meaning and understanding. Explain that the next exercise is going to demonstrate this.

Activity 1 (20 minutes)

1. In advance, compose a list of sandwich fillings on a sheet of paper. The list should be relatively long (about 20 words), and some items on the list should be repeated, for example lettuce, egg, tomato, mayonnaise, egg, vegan cheese, ham, egg, pickles, chicken, olives, lettuce. Include foods to reflect diversity within the group and different dietary requirements, plus one or two things they may not be so familiar with that may be harder to remember during the exercise.

2. To play, ask the children to sit comfortably and listen. Then announce, 'Today I made a special sandwich with...' then read out the list of sandwich fillings at a steady pace. Immediately afterwards hand each child an A4 piece of paper and a pen. They now have one minute to draw the sandwich with as many fillings as they can remember.

3. Call time and repeat the sentence followed by the sandwich list again, this time asking the children to tick the filling on their picture as it is called out. From experience, most will remember the repeated words, and several will write down words related to sandwich making not actually on the list read out, such as bread, butter. At the end, instruct everyone to count the ticks to find out which children remembered the most.

4. Suggest that this exercise demonstrates something called 'selective listening', which means hearing and interpreting parts of a message that seem familiar, relevant or interesting to you, while forgetting, ignoring or overlooking the rest. Explain that this can happen in conversations too, where we think we know what someone is going to say so stop listening and either complete it in our heads or butt in to finish the sentence, sometimes incorrectly. This miscommunication can be frustrating and even lead to arguments, as everyone likes to be heard and valued for what they say.

Activity 2 (15 minutes)

1. Explain that being a good listener is an important part of friendship. Learning how to actively listen means concentrating on what is being said, giving your full attention and waiting for the other person to stop before replying.

2. Demonstrate by splitting the group into pairs. Explain that each child will take turns to listen to their partner telling them in detail how to make their favourite sandwich. Once both have spoken, invite them to share back what

they heard. This should see an improvement in the detail remembered, but suggest they try some other active listening skills to show they are engaged and understanding, such as:

- simple non-verbal signals, like nodding, to show someone has got it right

- reflecting information back to check out understanding: 'You like cheese sandwiches best, but only cheddar?'

- displaying open body language to encourage someone to continue talking, for example sitting in a relaxed way, without crossing arms or covering the face

- asking questions: 'Who makes the best cheese sandwich at home?'

3. Bring the children back into a seated circle to take turns in introducing their partner, first by name and then by sharing what their favourite sandwich is. Explain that the ability to summarize information in this way is another active listening technique, which can be used to demonstrate that you fully understand what has been said. For example, 'This is Louella. She likes peanut butter and jam sandwiches on white bread best.'

Review (5 minutes)

1. Facilitate one last round of the circle, this time inviting each child to suggest a reason why listening is such an important component of a healthy friendship.

LESSON 2: EFFECTIVE COMMUNICATION IN RELATIONSHIPS

Aim

This lesson considers verbal and non-verbal styles of communication that might be used in different types of relationship, and the importance of assertiveness in expressing wishes and needs.

Learning outcomes

- Understand the importance of effective communication in relationships.

- Identify different verbal and non-verbal forms of communication.

- Recognize the difference between passive, assertive and aggressive communication styles.

Time: 70 minutes

Resources

- Whiteboard and markers

- A set of the Activity 1: Communication Cards

- Three A4 sheets of paper headed 'Passive', 'Assertive' and 'Aggressive'

- Activity 3: Communication Statements

How to do it
Introduction (5 minutes)

1. Introduce the topic by playing a quick word-association game by calling out the word 'communication' and then asking each child to suggest a different way they could communicate with someone. Record ideas up on the whiteboard.

2. Sum up that there are many different forms of communication, both verbal and non-verbal and that in this lesson you are going to explore ways that these can be used to communicate effectively with people.

Activity 1: (15 minutes)

1. Explain that in this exercise the children are going to explore ways that we can show others how we feel without any words being spoken.

2. Form a circle, giving an Activity 1: Communication Card to each of the children. Explain that on each card is a description of a feeling or emotion.

3. Invite a volunteer to step into the middle of the circle and give them one of the Communication Cards. On the word 'Go!' their task is to silently role-play the emotion on their card, while the other children try to guess what it is. A guess can be made at any stage in the process. If the feeling or emotion is correctly identified, the child should swap places with the current role-player to act out what is on their own card. If they are wrong, play continues until someone gets it right.

4. The game ends when everyone has had the opportunity to express non-verbal communication. Facilitate a review to consider which feelings and emotions were easiest to communicate to others and which were easiest to see in others.

5. Suggest that some might be confusing as they present in similar ways, for example feeling tired and feeling bored. Mistaking one for the other could lead to people feeling misunderstood, hurt or frustrated. This in turn could lead to arguments, conflict and ultimately relationships breaking down, so it is important to check out meaning and then respond accordingly.

Activity 2 (10 minutes)

1. Introduce the children to three styles of communication: passive, assertive and aggressive by passing the word 'No' around the class, starting timidly in a passive way and building up through confident assertiveness to increasing levels of aggression and finally shouting it out.

2. Explore how these different types of communication may look, sound and feel, both as a communicator and to the person on the receiving end:
Passive:

   ▣ No eye contact and looking down at the floor.

   ▣ Speaking so quietly that you can't be heard.

   ▣ Not saying what you think, feel or need.

   ▣ Going along with others, even when you don't want to.
   Assertive:

   ▣ Making eye contact.

- Speaking with confidence.

- Respecting your own and other people's right to speak and be heard.

- Using 'I' statements to say what you think, feel or need.
Aggressive:

- Being rude or bossy.

- Speaking loudly over the top of others.

- Invading other people's space.

- Only talking about your own wants and needs.

Activity 3 (30 minutes)

1. Take the pre-prepared A4 headed sheets of paper and lay them equidistantly in a line on the floor to create a continuum; 'Passive', 'Assertive' and 'Aggressive'.

2. Read out the list of Activity 3: Communication Statements. After each statement, the children should move to the point on the continuum they think reflects the style of communication demonstrated. Encourage the children to look around to compare ideas, asking for individuals to share their decision-making process. Where there is a difference of opinion, explore why.

3. Enable the children, in pairs, to practise speaking assertively to each other by taking it in turns to work through the following dilemmas:
Dilemma 1: Your friend asks you to play outside, but you prefer to continue what you are doing on your device inside.

   Dilemma 2: You are discussing what colour to paint your bedroom with a parent. They suggest green, but you want it painted in your favourite colour, which isn't the same.

4. Afterwards review:

   - How easy is it to remain assertive and say what you really want?

   - How did the other person react?

   - Were you happy with the outcome? Why/why not?

5. Reiterate that assertive communication means saying what you want, being clear in your message and setting boundaries, all while respecting others' right to a different opinion. Being assertive does not mean that you always get what you want but it ensures that your message is understood and is less likely to lead to conflict than being passive, where people can

feel overlooked and unheard, or being aggressive, where communications can escalate into arguments.

Review (10 minutes)

1. Demonstrate assertive communication by passing the word 'No' one more time around the circle. This time invite the children to add a context, for example, 'No thank you, I do not want any more food.'

2. Conclude that assertive communication is usually the best way to be heard and have your rights acted on, while showing respect to others.

ACTIVITY 1: COMMUNICATION CARDS

Feeling scared	**Feeling brave**	**Feeling anxious**
Feeling happy	**Feeling sad**	**Feeling proud**
Feeling cold	**Feeling lonely**	**Feeling hungry**

Feeling shy	**Feeling lost**	**Feeling kind**
Feeling excited	**Feeling bored**	**Feeling tired**
Feeling confident	**Feeling angry**	**Feeling embarrassed**

Feeling disappointed

Feeling frustrated

Feeling ashamed

Feeling hot

Feeling left out

Feeling appreciated

Feeling uncertain

Feeling bold

Feeling awkward

Feeling in control

Feeling small

Feeling jealous

Feeling friendly

Feeling blamed

ACTIVITY 3: COMMUNICATION STATEMENTS

1. Shrugging and refusing to say how I really feel (passive)

2. Speaking clearly and confidently (assertive)

3. Finding it hard to say 'no' when I don't want to do something (passive)

4. Owning up and apologizing when I do something wrong (assertive)

5. Shouting over the top of others when they are talking (aggressive)

6. Allowing people to talk over me (passive)

7. Being willing to compromise if agreement can't be reached (assertive)

8. Blaming others when things go wrong (aggressive)

9. Pretending I like something to fit in (passive)

10. Making scary faces to frighten others (aggressive)

11. Making myself small in the hope no one will ask me (passive)

12. Respecting other people's views (assertive)

13. Getting angry and hitting out (aggressive)

14. Banging the door shut behind me in an argument (aggressive)

15. Taking it in turns to talk and listen (assertive)

16. Saying nothing is wrong when it is clear I am upset (passive)

17. Pointing my finger at people when I'm angry (aggressive)

18. Standing too close to intimidate someone (aggressive)

19. Letting someone finish even if I don't agree with them (assertive)

20. Having to have the last word every time (aggressive)

LESSON 3: HEALTHY AND UNHEALTHY FRIENDSHIPS

Aim

This lesson helps children to consider what makes a healthy friendship and to identify indicators of a less healthy one, including peer pressure.

Learning outcomes

- Identify the difference between healthy and unhealthy friendships.

- Recognize different forms of peer pressure and tactics that might be used to coerce, encourage or bully someone into doing something.

- Identify ways to be assertive and resist peer pressure.

Time: 70 minutes

Resources

- Sets of the Activity 1: Friendship Cards

- Plastic bottle of water

- A set of the Activity 2: Pressure Bottle Cards

- Clock to time each role play

How to do it
Introduction (5 minutes)

1. Open the lesson by recapping the importance of friendship to emotional wellbeing and some of the skills and qualities that make someone a good friend. These include trust, respect, loyalty and honesty.

Activity 1 (25 minutes)

1. Seat the children around tables in small groups of four to six. Place a set of Activity 1: Friendship Cards in the middle of each table. Explain that each card has a different statement on it relating to friendship and the group task is to discuss each of the statements and then decide if they think it describes a positive, healthy aspect of a friendship, or something that is

negative, unhealthy or dangerous. Once agreed, cards can be placed in two piles, 'healthy' or 'unhealthy'. If they are struggling to decide, suggest that testing the statement by asking, 'Is this something a true friend would do or say?' should help.

2. Allow time for discussion, then invite a volunteer from each group to select and read out a statement they have placed on their healthy relationship pile, encouraging them to share their reasons why and promoting discussion where decisions vary. Once all of the positives have been identified, ask the children to share the cards from their 'unhealthy' pile. Again, ask the children to clarify how or why they feel it is negative and speculate on the potential consequences for everyone in the scenario.

3. Conclude that in a positive friendship each person maintains their outside interests and enjoys family time or being with other friends, as well as enjoying the time they spend together. Healthy friendships are based on mutual trust, respect and kindness, where people want the best for each other, rather than becoming upset, jealous or angry if a friend chooses to do things independently. Suggest that good friends listen to each other and respect each other's opinions, likes and wishes – even if they do not share them. Equally, all friendships have disagreements, but these can usually be resolved by talking honestly and listening to each other to find a solution. If this doesn't work, or if anyone is putting on pressure, using threats or becoming aggressive to get their own way, it is time to get help from a trusted adult.

Activity 2 (30 minutes)

1. This is a role-play activity where two children at a time play out a short scenario while the others watch and then comment on what they have seen before directing an assertive response.

2. Start by asking for two volunteers. Give Child 1 a bottle of water and Child 2 an Activity 2: Pressure Bottle Card. Each card outlines a different technique for persuading someone to do what you want. Explain that Child 2 has two minutes (maximum) to persuade Child 1 to give them the bottle, using the persuasion style assigned on the card. They cannot use any physical contact and they are not allowed to snatch the bottle.

   Top tip: Make sure only the child playing the Pressure Bottle Card knows what's on it.

3. Meanwhile, Child 1 should do their best to resist the pressure being applied and try to keep the water for themselves. At any point they can hand over the bottle if: a) they are persuaded that Child 2 should have the water or b) they cannot resist the pressure Child 2 is applying any longer.

4. After two minutes, call time and invite the rest of the children to review what they have just seen. Ask them to guess what sort of pressure was being used (emotional, charm, bullying etc.) and how effective it was. If Child 2 was successful in persuading Child 1 to give them the bottle of water, explore how and why they gave it up. Move on to review the strategies used by Child 1 to resist the peer pressure Child 2 was applying to keep the water. Was it successful? How did it feel to deny Child 2 what they wanted? What else could they have done?

5. Acknowledge that some individuals find it easier than others to be assertive. Suggest that practising being assertive can help build the skills to resist peer pressure in real life and ask for examples of assertive behaviour. These could include:

   ▢ standing up straight and making eye contact

   ▢ saying 'No' firmly and repeating it as necessary

   ▢ avoiding apologizing (e.g. 'Sorry, but I'm not sharing my water.')

   ▢ using confident body language that reflects what is being said

   ▢ walking away

   ▢ telling someone or asking for help.

Review (10 minutes)

1. Conclude by asking each child to identify one characteristic of a healthy friendship (e.g. loyalty, respect, kindness) and one characteristic that might alert someone to an unhealthy friendship (e.g. bullying, peer pressure, unkindness).

2. Remind the children that while all friendships have their ups and downs, and friends do not always agree, it is never right to put pressure on someone, or try to force them to do something using emotional or physical force. Being assertive and sticking to your boundaries can help but if anyone ever feels anxious, worried or that too much pressure is being put on them, they should ask for help from a trusted adult.

Extension activity

Consider other situations where someone might try to persuade a peer to do something (e.g. doing something they know to be unsafe, unfair or unkind). Role-play some of these, using the assertiveness tips discussed to build confidence.

A friend taking charge and making all the decisions for both of you.	Sticking up for your friend in front of others.	Thinking your friend doesn't like you if they want to spend time with someone else.
Joining in with bullying and unkind comments on social media.	Feeling scared to ask your friend to give something back they borrowed.	Feeling proud of your friend's achievement as well as your own.
Sitting quietly with a friend when they are feeling sad rather than going out to play with others.	Getting angry when your friend doesn't want to play the same game as you.	Pressuring your friend into telling lies to get you out of trouble.

Being too scared to tell someone that you don't want to be their friend anymore.

Shoving or hitting your friend when you argue.

Sharing embarrassing photos on social media without asking permission.

ACTIVITY 2: PRESSURE BOTTLE CARDS

Asking politely (e.g. Please can I have?)

Asking aggressively (e.g. Give it to me)

Using flattery (e.g. You are such a nice friend, I'm sure you will share)

Blame (e.g. It's your fault I forgot to bring my water)

Emotional blackmail (e.g. If you were a real friend you would want to share)

Threatening (e.g. If you don't give me your water, I'm going to hurt you)

Reasoning (e.g. It is only fair that you share, after all we both need a drink)

Guilt (e.g. If I die of thirst, it will be your fault)

Anger (e.g. Do as I ask, or I will get angry)

**Begging
(e.g. Please, please, please let me have some)**

**Bargaining
(e.g. If you say yes, you can use my phone)**

**Deceiving
(e.g. My water will be here in a minute)**

**Call to loyalty
(e.g. You said we would share everything, now you are going back on it)**

**Call to others
(e.g. What will your mum say when she finds out how selfish you are?)**

LESSON 4: GENDER STEREOTYPES

Aim

This lesson introduces the concept of gender stereotypes, what they are, where they come from, and the potential impact they can have on relationships.

Learning outcomes

- Recognize that stereotypes are assumptions applied to a whole group of people with shared common characteristics, rather than based on facts.

- Understand that stereotypes can be unfair, negative and impact on thoughts, actions and behaviour.

- Discover ways to identify and challenge gender stereotypes.

Time: 90 minutes

Resources

- Sets of the Activity 1: Gender Stereotype Cards

- Internet access (to research superheroes)

- Art supplies (coloured pencils, felt tip and marker pens)

- Large sheets of paper

How to do it
Introduction (15 minutes)

1. Read this short story and then ask the children the questions underneath:

    It is a hot day, and two children are paddling their feet in a play pool in the garden. One is reading a book quietly, but the other is bored so decides to play a trick. They fill a bucket with cold water and empty it into the pool, deliberately soaking their friend's pink t-shirt and splashing their book. Chuckling loudly and pleased with their prank, they scramble to their feet and run away shouting, 'Catch me if you can!'

    Questions:

    - How many children are there in the story?

- How many boys were reading a book?

- How many girls had a wet t-shirt?

- How many boys and how many girls were shouting?

2. Invite the children to raise their hands to answer each question, remarking on the most popular answers. Wait until the end to point out that the only question that has a definitive answer in this story, is that there were two children. The answers to the other questions are all unknown as the whole story is non-gender specific. If the children have given gendered answers, ask them how they came to their conclusion. It is likely that any answers given were based on gender stereotypes, for example girls wear pink t-shirts, boys are more likely to play tricks.

3. Define stereotypes as assumptions made about what someone does or how they behave based on the groups they belong to, such as gender, race or faith. For example, girls like reading quietly; boys enjoy playing pranks. The facts are that some children like quiet play more than active games and some like pink t-shirts while others prefer blue, regardless of gender.

Activity 1: (20 minutes)

1. Divide the class into small groups, giving each group a set of Activity 1: Gender Stereotype Cards. The task is to discuss and then sort each card into two categories: 'Stereotype' and 'Not a Stereotype'.

2. After sorting, go through each of the Gender Stereotype Cards, inviting groups to take turns in sharing which category they chose and why. Suggest that not challenging gender-based stereotypes can limit individual aspirations, meaning that people do not reach their full potential. Select a few of the stereotypes outlined on the cards to openly challenge. For example, challenge the stereotype that girls are not brave and adventurous with the story of Amelia Earhart,[1] who made history in 1932 as the first woman to complete a transatlantic solo flight, or Dame Ellen MacArthur,[2] who in 2005 became the fastest solo sailor to sail around the world. Point out that achievements like this take courage and bravery, which are not gendered qualities.

Activity 2: (20 minutes)

1. Explain that stereotypes can originate from a wide variety of sources, including TV and films, social media, family, friends and personal

---

1 https://kids.nationalgeographic.com/history/article/amelia-earhart
2 www.ellenmacarthurfoundation.org/about-us/ellens-story#:~:text=In%202005%2C%20Ellen%20MacArthur%20became,transition%20to%20a%20circular%20economy

experiences. Being able to identify a stereotype and understand where it comes from can help to challenge and break them effectively.

2. Task the children in small groups to go online and research 'superheroes'. Give them paper and pens to make notes of what stereotypes they discover in terms of gender, ethnicity, age and body size/shape and abilities. They can record their findings under the headings 'Male Superheroes' and 'Female Superheroes'. For example, are most of the male superheroes the same body shape? Do the majority of female superheroes wear a specific type of clothes?

3. Invite each group to present their findings. Explain how this can create, reinforce and perpetuate gender stereotypes. For example, the muscle-bound bodies of male superheroes reinforce the stereotype that men should be big and strong. Female superheroes often perpetuate stereotypes about beauty, with long flowing hair, small waists, big breasts and so on.

4. After everyone has shared their findings, facilitate a class discussion on the potential impact of gender stereotypes and how they can negatively affect people's self-esteem and opportunities. For example, if masculinity is depicted in the media (including superheroes) as tall, strong and muscly, how might it feel to be a man or boy who doesn't fit this narrow ideal? Suggestions could include: embarrassed, worried or anxious about your body, less masculine.

5. Challenge the stereotype, taking the opportunity to remind the children that there is no such thing as a 'perfect' body shape. Everyone grows at different rates and things like genetics (e.g. how tall your biological parents are), diet and physical health, exercise and even ethnicity all play a part in how muscly or physically strong someone is. Point out that superheroes often have other qualities that make them special, such as loyalty, respect and determination to help others, which make them a positive role model.

Activity 3 (30 minutes)

1. Give out large sheets of paper and art supplies. The task is for each child to create their own superhero, based on themselves. This should ignore the gender stereotypes identified in the previous activity to capture their personality and the skills and qualities that make them special, both externally and internally. They can also choose a superhero name and one superpower, which can be similar to an existing superhero or a totally new power they have made up.

2. When all the pictures are complete, display to create a 'Wall of Heroes'. Facilitate gallery time so that each child can introduce theirs, including the superpower they have chosen and how they would use it to benefit others.

Review (5 minutes)

1. Reflect on what has been learned, starting with gender stereotypes related to colours through to superheroes. Suggest that believing these stereotypes can limit choices, emotions and behaviour in real life. For example, boys thinking it isn't masculine to cry, or girls believing it isn't feminine to be brave and adventurous. This can then impact on how people behave within relationships and when making friendship choices, perhaps having expectations about what activities they enjoy and making assumptions about the movies and music they will like, and so on.

2. Stress the importance of doing the things you love, wearing the colours that make you happy, and setting goals for the things that motivate and inspire you, regardless of gender, rather than conforming to a stereotype that may not represent who you really are.

ACTIVITY 1: GENDER STEREOTYPE CARDS

Blue is a boy's colour	**Girls can't play rugby**	**Boys are natural leaders**
Girls are more caring	**Boys are better at science**	**Girls like cooking more than boys**
Boys are naturally better at puzzles	**Girls are naturally good homemakers**	**Boys are less emotional than girls**

Girls love pink and purple sparkly things

Boys don't like reading books

Girls are not brave or adventurous

Boys are naturally aggressive

Girls talk more than boys do

Boys are not interested in art or creativity

All girls want to be wives and mothers

LESSON 5: FOLLOW THE CROWD

Aim

The activities in this lesson plan explore the power of peer pressure and consider the potential consequences of following the crowd in a range of situations.

Learning outcomes

- Understand the roles people take in friendship groups.

- Understand the potential for losses and gains of giving in to peer pressure.

- Explore the potential consequences of resisting peer pressure.

Time: 90 minutes

Resources

- Copies of the Activity 1: Follow the Crowd Worksheet

- Pens and large sheets of paper

- Copies of the Activity 2: Follow the Crowd Scenarios

How to do it
Introduction (15 minutes)

1. Start with a quick game of 'Simple Simon', where children follow a set of instructions prefaced with the words 'Simple Simon says' but stand still if the instruction is given alone. Invite different children to lead the game to experience both giving instructions and following them.

2. Suggest that while it might not be as clear as it is in this game, in most friendship groups individuals play a role, including leader.

Activity 1 (20 minutes)

1. Ask the children to share an example of a time where they were prompted to do something because a friend did it. This could be something that was recommended, like listening to a specific song, reading a book, watching a film or downloading an app, or something bigger like joining an after-school

club, supporting a sports team or wearing the same clothes to show solidarity or which friendship group they associate with. Suggest that while this can be a positive thing there is a less positive side too, which can lead people into doing things they may regret or behaving in ways that have negative consequences for themselves or others.

2. Hand out the Activity 1: Follow the Crowd Worksheet and a pen to each child. Ask them to read each of the scenarios on the worksheet and then write a few words to describe the potential benefits or drawbacks of the consequences for going along with it. For example, if someone writes their names on a wall and you decide to join in, the 'benefit' might be that you become accepted by that group, but the 'drawbacks' could include being seen and reported to your parents, or the police.

3. When everyone has completed their sheet, bring the children back together to discuss their findings for each scenario. Ask:

'What might be the pressures to go along with something, even if you don't want to, or know it to be wrong?'

Ideas could include being left out of the peer group, being laughed at, mocked or thought a coward for not joining in, arguments or even bullying.

'What might be the benefits of not joining in?'

Suggestions could include, being true to your own values, not getting into trouble, being respected, prompting others to think about what they are about to do and potentially making a different decision.

4. Reinforce the benefits of having all of the information and considering the consequences of different choices before making a decision.

Activity 2 (40 minutes)

1. Divide the children into groups of six, allocating each group one of the Activity 2: Follow the Crowd Scenarios. Read the scenarios first and select those most age-appropriate. Explain that everyone will play an active part in devising a short scene to explore the potential outcomes of giving in to peer pressure before coming up with a resolution that resists it. Hand out paper and pens to record ideas.

2. The format is to role-play the three characters in the scenario, up to the point where peer pressure is being applied. At this point, another group member will call 'Freeze frame', whereby the action must stop, and while the three actors hold their pose, other members of the group will move around them, sharing aloud the potential consequences of giving in and

going ahead. On the call of 'Freeze frame' for the second time, the action should restart, this time using the strategy (or strategies) agreed for resolving the issue and any tensions created. The scene ends when all three characters agree a choice of action that keeps them safe and free of any of the negative consequences identified.

3. Allow up to 20 minutes for each group to decide which of them will play the three characters in their scenario, who will call 'Freeze frame' and who will form the chorus that narrates the consequences, before planning the storyline and ways to resist this form of peer pressure, which will direct the ending.

4. Ask each group to perform their role-play, leading a round of applause after each one. Allow time for comments, suggestions and questions, which the group role-playing the scenario should answer, before inviting the next group to perform theirs.

5. In particular, focus on the strategies for resolution, recognizing that it is sometimes hard to do the right thing, especially if that means going against what a friend wants. Conclude by pointing out that friends should not attempt to charm, coerce or bully each other into doing something they are uncomfortable with, or that they have said no to. Make it clear that 'no' always means no.

Review (15 minutes)

1. Facilitate a circle time activity using the following scenarios to practise saying no and making positive decisions to resist peer pressure. Keep answers short, reminding the children that in most situations you only have a few seconds to think about it and respond. Suggest that practising like this can help when it comes to real-life dilemmas.

   ▣ A friend makes unkind remarks about a classmate and expects you to join in.

   ▣ You are forwarded a social media picture that others are making fun of and asked to add your comment.

   ▣ Someone has stolen alcohol from home and passes it to you to try.

   ▣ You are being pressured to stay out later than your curfew.

   ▣ Your friends are making fun of the sports team you support, pressing you to change to theirs.

   ▣ You have a friend round and they suggest you both take extra chocolate biscuits without asking.

- A friend has a vape and invites you to have a go.

- Your friends are laughing at a spiteful joke.

- An older sibling is asking you to lie to your parents for them.

- Your friend wants you to choose the same t-shirt as them, but you like something else better.

ACTIVITY 1: FOLLOW THE CROWD WORKSHEET

Think about the potential benefits and drawbacks of joining in:

1. Joining in when other children laugh at someone falling over.

   Benefits . . . .

   Drawbacks . . . .

2. Siding with children you don't really like instead of sticking up for a friend.

   Benefits . . . .

   Drawbacks . . . .

3. Joining in with a friend who is messing about in class and not listening to the teacher.

   Benefits . . . .

   Drawbacks . . . .

4. Repeating a lie a friend has told to get out of trouble at home.

   Benefits . . . .

   Drawbacks . . . .

5. Staying out to play with friends later than you are allowed.

   Benefits . . . .

   Drawbacks . . . .

6. Joining in with children who knock on neighbours' doors then run away for a joke.

   Benefits . . . .

   Drawbacks . . . .

7. Going along with friends who refuse to own up to something, despite knowing others will be unfairly punished.

   Benefits . . . .

   Drawbacks . . . .

ACTIVITY 1: FOLLOW THE CROWD WORKSHEET

ACTIVITY 2: FOLLOW THE CROWD SCENARIOS

Scenario 1

Characters: Sol, Meghan and Destiny

Destiny: Hey, have you seen 'The Dare Challenge' on social media? We should do one together!

Sol: Isn't that where they set each other crazy dares? I saw a kid do a massive jump, and another where someone had to eat disgusting stuff – isn't it dangerous?

Meghan: Yes, I guess so, but you can make loads of money if your challenge is popular, so it's probably worth it.

Destiny: Stop worrying, the social media platform wouldn't allow it if it was that dangerous. What shall we do as our challenge?

Freeze frame

Scenario 2

Characters: Natasha, Flo and Cleo

Flo: Hey girls, I met this older boy who hangs out with his friends in town. He is amazing and makes our friends look so childish. He asked me to bring my best girls to a party on Friday, want to come?

Natasha: Sounds like fun, I find it much easier to be with an older group, they don't treat me like a baby.

Cleo: How much older? Why don't they want to hang out with girls their own age? I'm not sure it's a good idea.

Flo: Don't be silly! He's only a couple of years older and girls mature faster than boys. The age gap doesn't matter.

Freeze frame

Scenario 3

Characters: Harry, Shaun and Rollo

Rollo: I found some alcohol in my stepbrother's bedroom, so I took it for us to drink. Why don't you two steal some from home too? Then we can have our own party with no adults around to tell us what to do!

Harry: That sounds like a good plan – I am fed up being bossed around, let's go to the woods and have some fun!

Shaun: Hang on, what happens if things go wrong, or someone gets sick? If we are in the woods, no one will know where we are to send help.

Rollo: Go wrong? What could go wrong? Everyone drinks alcohol, don't try to spoil the fun by worrying about bad things that will never happen.

Freeze frame

Scenario 4

Characters: Molly, Ben and Milo

Milo: I dare you to go into that empty house; it's supposed to be haunted.

Molly: I'm not scared of ghosts but what if someone calls the police? We will get into trouble for trespass, and the police are bound to call our parents.

Ben: You are such a baby, Molly! I bet you are scared of ghosts, that's why you're saying all that stuff about the police – you're just trying to put us off.

Milo: Molly, if you can't accept a dare, I don't think you are brave enough to be our friend.

Freeze frame

Scenario 5

Characters: Ruby, Clyde and Rueben

Ruby: Wow! I've just seen this new diet online. All you need to do is take this supplement with your normal meals and you lose loads of weight in weeks.

Clyde: I've seen that too, it looks amazing. Apparently, it is based on an ancient recipe that was a closely guarded secret for years.

Rueben: But how do you know it's safe? If it's not prescribed by a doctor, you could be taking anything.

Ruby: Who cares? This is an easy way to get healthy without trying.

Freeze frame

LESSON 6: THE POWER OF APOLOGY

Aim

This lesson explores the importance of being able to recognize how personal actions and decisions can impact negatively on others. It also emphasizes the importance of building empathy and learning to acknowledge wrongdoing and apologize.

Learning outcomes

- Understand the importance of taking responsibility for personal actions and knowing when to apologize.

- Recognize the potential impact on relationships of not acknowledging harm done.

- Understand the link between words and actions to reduce the likelihood of repeated or future conflict.

Time: 90 minutes

Resources

- Copies of the Activity 2: Not Saying Sorry Worksheet (one for each child)

- Pens

- Sets of the Activity 3: Apology Scenario Cards (one set per group of three)

- Copies of the Activity 3: Observer Feedback Sheet (three cards per group of three)

How to do it
Introduction (15 minutes)

1. Play a word game called '101 Reasons Why my Homework Didn't Get Done'. Explain that this is a fun rather than serious activity, where each child listens to the reason the person in front of them gives before coming up with their own excuse. These can be pragmatic excuses, such as forgetting, but tend to get more imaginative as the game progresses. The only rule

is that each excuse must be prefixed with the words, 'Sorry but ...' For example, 'Sorry, but the dog ate it!'

2. Keep going with ever more outlandish excuses. If someone hesitates, or can't think of one, they are out.

3. The winner is the last person to contribute a reason. Congratulate them for their inventiveness, pointing out that no one is likely to believe such tall stories.

Activity 1 (15 minutes)

1. Summarize that the previous game highlighted that people often say 'sorry' when they are not really sorry at all. With the children in pairs or threes, invite them to talk about times when they have said sorry when they didn't really mean it. Ask them to practise and then share with the whole class impressions of saying the word 'sorry' when you don't mean it. As they do their impressions, invite the rest of the class to suggest clues that it is not a genuine apology, for example it sounds forced, grudging or sarcastic.

2. Move on to ask: 'Why do you think people say sorry when they aren't?'

   Reasons could include hoping to get into less trouble, because they think they should or it is expected, because they've been told to, and so on.

3. Conclude that apologies can be overused, which makes them less meaning-ful and harder to believe and it is more difficult to forgive any harm done.

Activity 2 (20 minutes)

1. Give each child a copy of the Activity 2: Not Saying Sorry Worksheet and a pen. The worksheet sets out a range of situations. Their task is to consider what could happen if the main character chooses not to apologize. Allow time to complete individually and then move the children into small groups to share and compare answers.

2. Bring the whole class together to reflect on the importance of an apology, even if any harm caused was accidental or the consequence of owning up is still going to be a punishment (e.g. for taking something that isn't yours or breaking a boundary). Suggest that lying to get out of trouble or blaming someone else is never the right thing to do and could lead to long-term damage to a relationship (e.g. loss of trust). Even punishments are usually smaller if you own up rather than wait to get caught or found out, as the truth and a meaningful apology are valued and show that someone is able to take responsibility.

Activity 3 (25 minutes)

1. Ask: 'How do we know when someone is really sorry?'

   Suggestions could include genuine remorse shown, non-verbal communication like making eye contact, tone of voice, other emotions displayed that show they are upset or empathize.

2. Explain that the children are now going to have the opportunity to put this into practice, based on the series of scenarios from Activity 3: Apology Scenario Cards, which they are going to role-play. For each scenario, one or more apologies could improve the situation, reducing the potential for the conflict to escalate, but it is up to the children to work out how. With the children working in groups of three, assign roles, with one person acting as an observer to give feedback afterwards. There is an Activity 3: Observer Feedback Sheet for them to make notes on to give feedback afterwards.

3. Allow three to five minutes for each role-play and then swap roles so that all three children in a group get to experience giving and receiving an apology, as well as observing one.

Review (15 minutes)

1. Ask the children to consider the potential consequences of not saying sorry when you have done something wrong. For example:

   - Being thought rude

   - Being thought inconsiderate

   - Denying any harm caused

   - Hurting feelings.

2. Point out that without an apology, if you have done something wrong or made a mistake, a relationship is likely to be damaged. It is not always easy to make good choices and sometimes we all make mistakes and need to say sorry to others. Suggest that recognizing you have made a mistake shows that you are taking responsibility for your actions and behaviour, which makes your apology more credible and more likely to be accepted.

ACTIVITY 2: NOT SAYING SORRY WORKSHEET

Read the dilemmas below. For each decide what could happen, positive or negative, if the person does not say sorry.

	Situation	What could happen
1	Accidentally bumping into an elderly person in the street.	
2	Arriving home late for tea because you were too busy playing out.	
3	Laughing when a bully says something unkind about your friend.	
4	Treading on someone's foot by accident on the bus.	
5	Calling your sibling a 'cheat' when they beat you fairly in a game.	
6	Getting caught telling a lie to your teacher about why you haven't done your homework.	
7	Borrowing a toy, then accidentally breaking it.	
8	Sneaking sweets that don't belong to you at home.	
9	Taking a sip out of someone else's drink by mistake.	
10	Blaming a sibling for something you did to avoid being grounded.	

ACTIVITY 3: APOLOGY SCENARIO CARDS

Scenario 1
Ella and Daisy have been best friends for a long time. One day, Ella accidentally spills her water all over Daisy's painting. Daisy gets angry and shouts, she has been working hard all morning and now Ella has ruined it. How can this situation be improved?

Scenario 2
During a game of tag, Sofia pushes Ryan too hard by mistake and he falls over. The rest of the class see it happen and start laughing. Even though Ryan is her friend, Sofia giggles too. Ryan loses his temper and calls Sofia rude names. How can this situation be improved?

Scenario 3
Bernie and Alexis have an argument about who should be the leader of their class space project. Bernie secretly told their classmates to vote him as leader, but Alexis found out and is very upset. They never usually argue as their friendship is based on a shared love of spacecraft, astronauts and space missions. How can this situation be resolved?

ACTIVITY 3: OBSERVER FEEDBACK SHEET

Please observe the role-play and comment on the following:

Who apologized: . . . .

. . . .

Communication style used:. . . . .

. . . .

Non-verbal communication observed: . . . .

. . . .

Do you think it helped resolve things? If so, how; if not, why?

. . . .

. . . .

. . . .

. . . .

. . . .

. . . .

. . . .

. . . .

. . . .

. . . .

CHAPTER 5

Online Relationships and Being Safe

This final chapter combines two topic areas in the Relationships Curriculum: online relationships and being safe. Children grow up in a fast-paced digital world, and the lessons here encourage them to critically think about the decisions they make both as contributors and consumers of online material, with an emphasis on the importance of respect for others, including when posting anonymously.

They will also learn about staying safe online and how to recognize risks, harmful content and contact, including the message that people sometimes behave differently online and don't always tell the truth.

KEY WORDS
Digital citizen, social media, gaming, consent, online, offline, safe, respect-ful, risky, harmful, communication, friends, messaging, appropriate, inappropriate

LESSON 1: LEAVING A DIGITAL FOOTPRINT

Aim

The aim of this lesson is to discuss the place that digital media has in our collective lives and introduce the concept of the digital footprint this creates.

Learning outcomes

- Recognize that digital technology enables everyone to be a creator of media, not just a consumer.

- Know what a digital footprint is and how it is created.

- Understand the importance of being a responsible, respectful digital citizen.

- Recognize that a digital footprint is a permanent record.

Time: 70 minutes

Resources

- Whiteboard and markers

- Copies of the Activity 1: Digital Footprint Worksheet (one per child)

- Art supplies (coloured pencils, felt tip and marker pens)

- Copies of the Activity 2: Elsa's Digital Life Story

- Sticky notes

How to do it
Introduction (10 minutes)

1. Do a quick poll to find out how much digital technology the children have access to using a copy of the small grid below drawn up on a whiteboard. Make it clear that the devices do not have to belong to them, it could be digital technology that they share (perhaps with siblings), or use that belongs to others (e.g. parents/carers or school).

Type of device	Own	Share	Have access to
Mobile phone			
Laptop			
Tablet			
PC			
Games console			
Smart TV			
Other			

2. Reflect on this with the children, and compare the facts from this class poll with the statistics that 38 per cent of children aged five to seven in the UK have a mobile phone, rising to 97 per cent by the time they are 16–17.[1]

3. Conclude that most people in the UK, including children, have access to digital technology and so make daily decisions about the content they create and consume. Suggest that this is why it is important to understand how to be a responsible 'digital citizen' and the digital footprint you create.

Activity 1 (20 minutes)

1. Ask the children if they have heard the term 'digital footprint' and what they think it means. Offer this definition to clarify:

> A digital footprint is an imprint left behind by all your online activities, including things you see or search for; things you listen to, play or read; things you upload like photos and digital content plus anything you like, forward or send. It is also made up of the things that other people say, send or do to you online.

2. Set up tables with six to eight children seated around them to share the art supplies. Their task is to each complete Activity 1: Digital Footprint Worksheet to create a visual representation of their own personal digital footprint, filling the footprint shape with words or pictures to represent how they currently use digital technology. This might include, for example, gaming sites or apps they use, social media, the platform they use to watch movies as well as direct communication methods like texts and messaging apps.

3. Once complete, the children can share and compare what they have included with their peers at the table. Ask for examples from each table

---

1 For more 2023 UK statistics see www.statista.com/statistics/1252353/devices-used-to-go-online-by-children-in-the-uk

to create a whole class digital footprint on a large sheet of paper, which can be displayed, or the contents used to create a digital consumption graph to refer back to later.

Activity 2 (30 minutes)

1. Facilitate this either as a story-time activity, where Elsa's Digital Life Story is read aloud and the questions used to extend learning and understanding, or as a small group activity.

2. Facilitate a discussion based around these questions:

   ▣ Do you think that Elsa's digital footprint is normal for her age? Why/ why not? How might yours look when you are 16?

   Refer to the earlier poll of digital media used by the children to help them assess this, compared with the story of Elsa. It is likely that this will prompt a realization of additional digital footprints outside the platforms and devices identified earlier (e.g. photos shared by family).

   ▣ Do you think there is anything for Elsa to worry about if the college or an employer checks her digital footprint?

   For example, has she made good choices about the platforms she uses, the content she shares and things like her username, SexyElsa123? Ask the children to consider what first impressions her choices might give, rightly or wrongly.

   ▣ Is Elsa right to think that her digital past will disappear? Why/why not?

   Remind everyone that while they may forget things they do online, a digital footprint is permanent. This is why it is important to make as many positive choices as you can about what you say, do and post. If you have shared things that you don't want others to see, go back and delete them. They may not be completely gone but it will make it harder to find if they have been shared.

3. Conclude that a digital footprint is a personal snapshot of interests, communication and digital behaviour, which anyone using digital technology will have. However, it can be hard to remember exactly what your journey has been online, especially if you use it a lot on multiple platforms. Suggest that the younger you start, the more of an imprint you are likely to create, positive and negative, so it is important to be aware of and make safe, respectful choices about what you do, say and share.

4. With the children back in their groups, with sticky notes and pens, ask them to compose messages to Elsa with any advice they can give about improving her digital footprint and staying safe while enjoying social media. Bring the class together to share ideas, which could include the following:

- Adhering to age requirements, both on apps and online content.

- Only accepting friend/follow requests from people known in real life.

- Setting privacy tools so that information is not visible to the public and people need permission to tag you in posts.

- Turning off location settings so no one can see where you are.

- Assessing profile names to make sure they present you as you want to be seen.

- Resetting passwords and not sharing them.

- Not getting into online arguments or liking/sharing hurtful comments.

- Every time you post or upload content, asking yourself if you want it as a permanent record.

- Taking time out if you need to and asking for help if you are unsure about posting or sharing content.

Review (10 minutes)

1. Summarize that digital technology is evolving and will continue to do so all the time. That's why it is important to understand the digital footprint you leave and develop the skills, knowledge and understanding to use technology in a way that is safe, healthy and respectful.

2. Create a gallery wall with the children using the completed Digital Footprint Worksheets, interspersed with the sticky notes clustered into topics. This can be left on display to raise awareness with other children too.

ACTIVITY 1: DIGITAL FOOTPRINT WORKSHEET

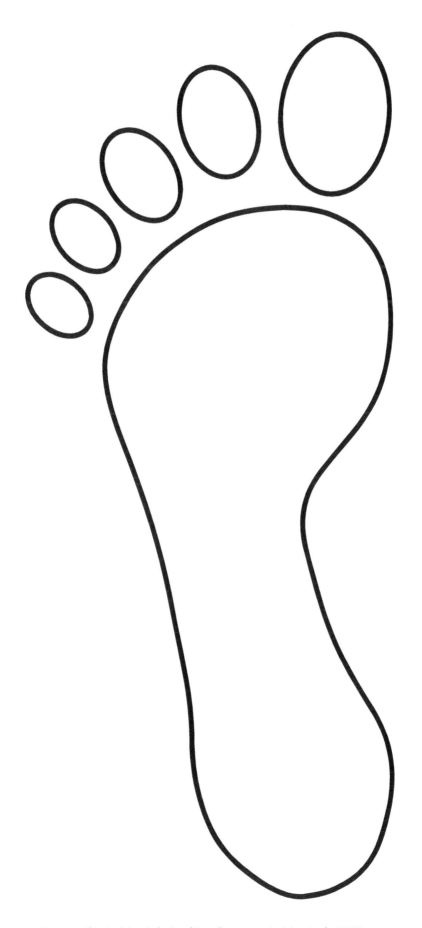

ACTIVITY 2: ELSA'S DIGITAL LIFE STORY

Elsa is 16 and plans to apply for college in September. She also wants a holiday job, and hopes to save some money before she goes. She knows that both the college and any potential employer are likely to look online to review her digital activity. This is her digital footprint so far:

Aged 0: Her mum shares her first pregnancy scan on social media with friends and family, so Elsa's digital footprint begins before she is born.

Aged 0–3 years: Elsa's proud parents, grandparents and other family members upload, share and re-post 973 photos and 137 videos of her. Elsa's mum and dad are digital savvy so have used privacy settings to limit who can see them. Her grandparents aren't, so they shared them with everyone they knew without any security or protection. This means that photos of Elsa may have been screenshot, shared or posted all over the internet without her knowledge or consent.

Aged 4–7 years: Elsa is allowed to play music and games on her parents' phones, which drives them increasingly mad, so she is given a tablet for her sixth birthday. Her parents thought they would be helping her navigate the internet so didn't set filters and parental controls. But Elsa has known since nursery how to do it, so she goes online to play games, talk to her friends and watch any content she chooses. This includes a clip of an 18R horror movie shared by her older sibling, which scares her so much she now sleeps with the lights on. She doesn't tell her parents the reason why.

Aged 8–12 years: Elsa has free texts with the mobile phone she gets for Christmas, but only uses them to talk to her parents, who don't know that she uses an encrypted messaging service to chat with friends. She spends hours in her bedroom on a video-sharing platform. She did use it in the living room, but it caused too many rows as the noise disturbed her parents who were working or relaxing in front of the TV. She also has a social media app, which she set up in her bedroom, so her parents don't know that Elsa lied about her age to create an account. Her friends all dare each other to send inappropriate photos, which they think is safe as they can be deleted. It isn't safe as several photos are screenshot, saved and shared on other platforms without Elsa knowing.

Aged 13–16 years: Elsa now has a tablet, a smart phone, a games console, a laptop (which her parents bought for schoolwork) and a smart TV in her bedroom. She spends most of her time there, chatting, posting and sharing photos with her 3000+ online friends, many of whom she has never met in the real world. She uses her email address as her username, SexyElsa123, on multiple platforms and enjoys it when she gets compliments on her heavily filtered selfie photos and videos. As a joke, she and a friend have created profiles on a dating app, lying about their age so that they can swipe left and right and send sexy messages to older men. Elsa loves the freedom social media gives her to say whatever she wants and be whoever she wants to be, unlike the real world where adults still set the rules.

To date, Elsa has never closed an old online account or taken down a social media profile. She thinks they will probably have disappeared by now as so much time has passed. There are photos out there that she hopes her parents never see but to be honest she stopped worrying about that a long time ago. The past is the past, right?

LESSON 2: THE IMPORTANCE OF CONSENT IN THE DIGITAL WORLD

Aim

This lesson encourages children to consider what they share about themselves and others online and the importance of permission-seeking before posting photos and other personal content. It aims to build their skills and confidence to be able to say both yes and no.

Learning outcomes

- Understand the meaning of consent in a range of circumstances.

- Understand the importance of consent in the making and sharing of digital content.

- Identify ways to set and maintain personal boundaries when using digital technology.

- Know what to do if you are concerned about content that is inappropriate, untrue or shared without permission.

Time: 125 minutes

Resources

- Whiteboard

- Sticky notes

- Six objects – these should be small, unrelated items (e.g. ball, sock, pen, flower, comb, teddy bear)

- Music (that can be started and stopped easily)

- Sets of the Activity 3: Consent Scenario Cards (enough for the children to work in groups of four or five)

- Props (hats, gloves, scarves and other costumes/props to role-play different characters)

- A Consent Review Sheet (one per child)

How to do it
Introduction (15 minutes)

1. Hand each child a wad of sticky notes and a pen. If possible, allocate a different coloured pen to each child. In the middle of the whiteboard, write the question: 'What does consent mean?'

2. Now ask the children to reflect independently on the question, writing down their ideas on the sticky notes.

3. Create a wordstorm by inviting the class, one child at a time, to come up to the whiteboard and stick their work around the question. Review the children's responses, reading the content of each sticky note aloud to assess shared understanding and challenge any misconceptions.

4. Conclude that consent means giving someone a choice about touch or actions and respecting the answer, even if you do not like it. Being able to ask for, give and receive consent is an important part of any relationship, both online and in the real world. Explain they will return to the wordstorm again at the end of the lesson.

Activity 1 (30 minutes)

1. Seat everyone in a circle and explain you are going to play a game called 'Pass the Object'. This is played a bit like pass the parcel, except that when the music stops the person holding the object must check if the person next to them is happy to receive it or chooses not to. If they decline, the object has to be offered to the person on the other side, who has the same options. If they also decline, the object is moved to another part of the circle and the game begins again.

2. As it progresses, gradually add new objects until all six are being passed around the circle. Stop play when everyone has had the opportunity to offer and decline an object.

3. Review by asking:

   - How easy/hard was it to accept or decline an object?

   - What influenced your choices?

   - Did you feel any pressure to accept?

   - Did is get easier/harder the more objects being passed around?

4. Recap that the game was based on the right to say yes or no, which we all have. Stress the importance of respecting this right, both online and in real life. Invite the children to share examples of where they may give, withhold or seek consent. Examples could be practical (e.g. having to ask

a teacher before leaving the classroom during lessons), or personal (e.g. being asked to lend something, physical touch or asking to join a game).

Activity 2 (20 minutes)

1. Remark that in the previous game, consent was given verbally. While verbal consent is very important there are other ways that permission can be given or refused, so it is important to be aware of not just how someone says something but also how they say it and things like body language. With the children working in pairs, ask them to come up with their own examples of ways to communicate consent without using any words. These could be things they have done themselves, seen others do, or heard about from real life or digital sources.

2. Allow five to ten minutes for conversations and then share back in the wider group to learn from each other. Here are some methods of communication:

   ▣ Non-verbal communication – for example, nodding a head to signal yes, or shaking it for no, giving a thumbs-up or -down.

   ▣ Body language – for example, open and enthusiastic or closed and withdrawn.

   ▣ Written – for example, a parent signing a consent form for a school trip, a reply to a birthday invitation.

   ▣ Online – for example, using an emoji to signal the answer, typing yes or no to a message request.

3. Positively reinforce all of the different suggestions, encouraging the children to role-play examples and emphasizing the importance of clear, explicit consent. Conclude that no means no, however it is conveyed, and this should be respected and acted on – even if you don't like the answer or wish it could be something else.

Activity 3 (45 minutes)

1. Divide the class into small groups of four to five children, with a set of Activity 3: Consent Scenario Cards, paper and pens. For each scenario, the children will need to discuss each of the characters, identify any potential online or real-life risks and then devise an appropriate response or plan of action to ensure that anything posted online or happening in real life is consensual. Alternatively, they could choose to only consent to some things and refuse for others. For example, in Scenario 2, Tom's brother Jack could consent to videos of his dancing being uploaded but only on one social media platform, or consent if the video only shows his feet dancing so his face is never seen.

2. Explain that it is completely up to each group to decide how the question of consent will be addressed and the outcome for each scenario, from which they will select one to devise a short scene lasting no more than three minutes, to be performed later. To capture their ideas, the children can write a script, storyboard or stage directions on the paper supplied.

3. Once this is agreed, the children can assign parts based on the characters in their chosen scenario, plus a narrator who will set the scene and give a short summary of why the group decided on this strategy to resolve the issues identified at the end. Give out props and costumes to help everyone get into character. When not acting, the rest of the group can take it in turns to be the:

   ▨ director – who directs the actors, provides feedback, encouragement and support during rehearsals, makes sure everyone is in the right place to start the performance and keeps the actors to time

   ▨ stage manager – who acts as support for the director and is responsible for the set, props, lights and costumes: for example, if the script requires the actors to be seated or the lights need to be turned down or off to symbolize night

   ▨ front of house – who liaises between the actors, the director and the stage manager, sets out or moves chairs for the audience, welcomes the audience before the performance and encourages audience participation and questions at the end.

4. Bring everyone back together and in turn invite each group to perform, followed by an opportunity (facilitated by the front of house) for the other groups to comment on the strategies for ensuring that everything is consensual and safe, and to ask questions. Afterwards, lead a round of applause and invite the children to throw off their assumed characters and rejoin the audience, ready to watch the next one.

5. Make sure the following points are addressed:

   ▨ Scenario 1: Mobile numbers and other contact details should only be shared with express consent. If, as in the scenario, someone asks for a friend's details, you should check with them first. If they are under 18 (or not the bill payer) they may need permission from a parent or guardian. If contact details are shared without permission, report and request them to be removed immediately as it is an offence under the Data Protection Act (2010). Everyone should be careful about who they give personal details to – whether this is to get free 'skins', or digital currency in gaming, responding to unsolicited messages about parcel deliveries or claiming prizes from competitions you don't remember entering – as they may be fraudulent or part of a wider scam.

▨ Scenario 2: Videos or any creative digital content should only be shared with the consent of the person making them, or if under 18, with parental consent. While in the scenario, the person wanting to upload the video has the best of intentions, this is not always the case. Sometimes films are secretly made and then shared to embarrass, shame, harass or hurt, which is a form of online bullying as well as being potentially illegal. If a video is uploaded without your permission, seek adult help to report it to the digital platform and ask them to remove it. If any content is potentially illegal or is likely to cause harm or increase vulnerability to grooming or exploitation, consider contacting police or reporting it (using your name or anonymously) to Child Exploitation and Online Protection (CEOP),[2] which offers free advice and the support of experienced child protection officers to help keep children safe online.

▨ Scenario 3: Posting photos without consent is unacceptable. You do not have to justify your reason for not wanting it posted, you can just ask the person who took it to remove it. If it is illegal or inappropriate content, tell a trusted adult and ask for help to get it removed from the platform. Contact the police if necessary.

▨ Scenario 4: In this scenario, a child sends an emoji representing a hug, which the receiver consents to accept by sending one back. In real life, physical contact should not take place without explicit consent. Hugging someone without consent could be considered a sexual assault. Ask first, 'You look in need of a hug, is it okay to give you one?' This provides the opportunity for the other person to either agree or say no. Any reluctance, silence or negative body language should always be perceived as a no.

Review (15 minutes)

1. Go back to the question that prompted the wordstorm: 'What does consent mean?' Recap what has been covered in the lesson, particularly that everyone has the right to say 'no', and the importance of respecting personal boundaries. Reinforce the message that if anyone is ever in doubt, feels concerned or even scared of something they see or are asked to do online or on social media, they should go to a trusted adult and ask for help. Make it clear that digital platforms have a responsibility to keep users safe too, and that they all offer a reporting system whereby posts can be taken

---

2   www.ceop.police.uk/Safety-Centre

down, users blocked, and accounts suspended or closed. Misuse can also be reported to the police, especially if accompanied by threats of violence, coercion or where there is evidence of grooming.

2. Give each child a pen and a Consent Review Sheet to complete, which enables them to reflect on their experiences and to identify new learning. These could be displayed, together with the consent wordstorm, to educate and inform others.

ACTIVITY 3: CONSENT SCENARIO CARDS

Scenario 1

Sarah is asked by a classmate to share Emma's mobile number. She wants to help but knows that Emma is not really friends with the person asking.

1. Is this a safe request?

2. What can Sarah do before sharing Emma's contact details?

3. Should anyone else be informed?

Scenario 2

Tom wants to upload a video of his brother Jack break-dancing to an online sharing platform. Tom thinks Jack is a brilliant dancer, but he is not sure how Jack will feel about potentially millions of people seeing him perform.

1. Is this safe to upload?

2. How can Tom make sure Jack is comfortable with it?

3. Will anyone else need to know?

Scenario 3

Sophie is scrolling through social media when she finds a picture of her friend Samira. She knows Samira isn't on this platform so can't have posted it herself. Sophie wonders if Samira knows her photo is out there.

1. Is this a safe situation?

2. How can Sophie find out if Samira agreed to her photo being shared?

3. Who else should be informed?

Scenario 4

River knows that Milly is sad so sends a virtual hug to comfort her. Milly sends one back and says she appreciates it. River sees Milly in school later and gives her a real-life hug too. He is sure that as she loved the virtual hug, she will be even happier with the real thing.

1. Is this safe to do?

2. What permissions has Milly given and not given?

3. How can River make sure Milly is comfortable with physical contact?

CONSENT REVIEW SHEET

Name . . . .

Consent means . . . .

. . . .

. . . .

. . . .

. . . .

Ways I can give or refuse it online or when using social media are . . . .

. . . .

. . . .

. . . .

. . . .

My personal boundaries should be respected because . . . .

. . . .

. . . .

. . . .

. . . .

It is important for me to respect other people's boundaries because . . . .

. . . .

. . . .

. . . .

. . . .

LESSON 3: HARMFUL COMMUNICATION ONLINE

Aim

This lesson promotes responsible communication when using digital technology, applying the same principles to online relationships as those in the real world. It explores the potential for harm to be caused by negative comments and builds empathy for the targets of online bullying.

Learning outcomes

- Understand what an online 'troll' is and the harm they cause online.

- Recognize the potential impact of posting unkind, untrue or unpleasant comments/content on self and others both online and in real life.

- Understand how to use the acronym THINK before posting or uploading content as a reminder of what constitutes appropriate content.

- Know how to report content that is inappropriate or harmful to providers.

Time: 120 minutes

Resources

- A template of a simple scalloped edged cloud shape (approximately 12cm long) and a similar size one of a spiky edged cloud shape. (Use the template to draw and cut out one copy of each shape per child.)

- Paper and scissors

- A wall to display work, separated into two areas under the headings 'Warm Glows' and 'Cold Prickles'

- A news item reporting on the effect of online 'trolls' (e.g. football players who receive online abuse,[3] or female politicians[4])

- Art supplies (coloured pencils, felt tip and marker pens)

- Large sheets of paper

---

3   https://talksport.com/football/1162478/man-utd-cristiano-ronaldo-harry-maguire-premier-league-twitter-instagram
4   https://theconversation.com/online-abuse-could-drive-women-out-of-political-life-the-time-to-act-is-now-214301

Teaching tip: If you do not have the time or resources to make your own cloud and spiky cloud shapes, consider using pre-cut large fluorescent paper star shapes (used in shops for 'sale' signs or to advertise prices on market stalls). These are widely available in a range of colours online or in high street stationers.

How to do it
Introduction (5 minutes)

1. Ask children to call out one-word descriptions of how they feel if someone does something kind or positive for them, and note these on the whiteboard – for example, happy, cared for, respected, grateful.

Activity 1 (45 minutes)

1. Introduce the idea that these positive feelings could be described as giving someone a 'warm glow'. Then ask the children how they feel if someone says or does something negative or unkind, and repeat the same process. Answers might include sad, angry, embarrassed, shamed or frightened. Suggest that a way of describing these feelings is a 'cold prickle'.

2. Explain that 'giving' warm glows to friends, family and even the wider community encourages the same behaviour in return, for example if someone smiles it is quite difficult not to smile back. Likewise, delivering a cold prickle can provoke an equally nasty response. Suggest that this is particularly true online, where things can quickly escalate into arguments and full-scale conflict, drawing everyone in. Point out that once a nasty comment is posted or a spiteful message sent, it is impossible to be 100 per cent certain who has seen, liked and shared it and there is no way of taking it back.

3. Hand each child a cloud- and prickle-shaped piece of paper and some coloured felt tip pens. On the soft, fluffy cloud-shaped piece of paper, ask them to write things they have seen, heard or watched online or on social media that they believe would produce a warm glow; for example, sending a smiley, happy emoji, complimenting a photo or sharing a video of a cute pet. Once they have written down their ideas, they can decorate the rest of the cloud in shapes and colours that provoke positive feelings and a sense of wellbeing.

4. On the cold prickle shape, ask the children to list online behaviour they think likely to provoke the opposite of a warm glow. For example, being harsh or over-critical, calling people nasty names, spreading gossip and lies or deleting someone from a friendship group, are all things that are likely to make someone feel hurt, lonely and unhappy. They can then decorate with shapes and colours to reflect how this feels too.

5. Once complete, invite the children to share and compare their work before creating a display under the headings 'Warm Glows' and 'Cold Prickles'.

Activity 2 (30 minutes)

1. Ask the children if anyone has heard the term 'online troll' and if so to describe what they think it means. Summarize that 'trolls' are named after the mythical beasts who lie in wait under dark bridges ready to jump out and scare or harm unsuspecting people, made famous in children's fairy stories. Online trolls remain anonymous but use social media platforms that allow public comments in a deliberate attempt to upset, provoke or anger someone they target. They may focus on one person but often choose several, using different platforms and multiple user accounts to bombard their chosen victim with negative comments so that it looks as if lots of people are engaging in the behaviour, rather than just one. This can go on for days or be sustained over many weeks or even months, leaving the victim feeling powerless to stop them.

2. Facilitate a discussion based on these questions:

   ▣ How might it feel to receive hundreds of 'cold prickles' a day?

   Suggestions could include feeling isolated, as though you have no friends; that you can't trust anyone as you don't know who is doing it; angry, especially if what they say is untrue; unheard, if it continues; that everyone is picking on you and there is no escape.

   ▣ Why might someone choose to be an online troll?

   Some trolls deliberately set out to provoke, shame or hurt someone they know but often they target a stranger to provoke a reaction or to get a sense of power and satisfaction from upsetting, offending, scaring or annoying someone. The target of a troll does nothing to 'deserve' this type of unwanted and unsolicited attention and should always be considered a victim.

3. Acknowledge all of the ideas the children suggest and then share the news item you have selected to demonstrate the negative impact of so-called online trolls. Point out that this can be directed against anyone, from high-profile victims (including sports heroes, actors and pop stars) to unknown individuals and sometimes their families too. This can have real-world impact, especially if threats to harm are made, creating fear and suspicion.

   ▣ What should you do if someone is targeting you in this way?

4. Encourage the children to problem-solve but when bringing everyone together to share and compare ideas, ensure that the following advice is included if anyone is targeted in this way:

▣ Don't respond – victims often want to appease or befriend the bully, hoping to solve the problem or calm things down. Others retaliate by sending their own negative comments or threats. However, responding can escalate the problem and make things worse.

▣ Block anyone leaving hurtful comments or threats. Consider deleting the profile that is being targeted for harm and creating a new one allowing only family and trusted friends to see it. Screenshot and save the evidence first.

▣ Report what has happened first to a parent/carer or other trusted adult who can offer support through the process of reporting it to the digital platform and/or the police. Explain that most schools have a zero-tolerance policy for this type of bullying behaviour, and that posting some content is illegal, including:

- explicit threats of violence to people or their property

- hate crime (protected characteristics)

- coercion

- harassment or stalking

- posting/sharing/forwarding inappropriate images.

Activity 3 (30 minutes)

1. Suggest that understanding how online behaviour can impact negatively on how people feel, and their emotional wellbeing, builds empathy to think about what we post before we post it.

2. Give out large sheets of paper to each child and make art supplies available to all. Their task is to create a poster that encourages other children to use the acronym THINK before posting or uploading digital content.

T = is it True?
H = is it Helpful?
I = is it Inspiring?
N = is it Necessary?
K = is it Kind?

3. Once they have completed the posters, invite the children to share their creations with the rest of the class, explaining their personal interpretation and why thinking in this way about what you post is important. Suggest that if it isn't at least one of these things, don't post it.

Review (10 minutes)

1. Recap on the learning so far, reinforcing the responsibility that every individual using social media or any other online platform has before they post, comment or livestream. Remind the children to tell an adult if anything makes them feel uncomfortable, scared or angry, and reiterate that all social media platforms have mechanisms to report inappropriate or harmful content. It can also be reported to the Child Exploitation and Online Protection Centre (CEOP) via its website,[5] and the police.

---

5   www.ceop.police.uk/Safety-Centre/CEOP

LESSON 4: CYBERBULLYING: BE AN UPSTANDER, NOT A BYSTANDER

Aim

This lesson explores different types of online bullying and discusses the difference between banter and bullying. It encourages children to be digital 'upstanders' and to report any form of online harm.

Learning outcomes

- Clarify the line between joking/friendly teasing and 'banter' that is hurtful and bullying.

- Understand different types of online bullying, and that these are wrong and unacceptable.

- Recognize what a digital upstander is and how to be one.

- Know where to go for support and how to report online bullying.

Time: 90 minutes

Resources

- Whiteboard, large sheets of plain paper and pens

- Sticky notes

- A bag (for collecting sticky notes)

- A copy of the Activity 1: Opinion Statements (this has prompt points to support facilitators)

- Copies of the Activity 3: The Role of a Bystander Worksheet (one per group of four to six children)

- Details of local support services for young people

How
Introduction (15 minutes)

1. In a seated circle, hand a sticky note and a pen to each child. Ask everyone to write down something that they think could be described as online

bullying or cyberbullying. For example: stalking, sending threatening messages, making hurtful comments or intentionally shaming someone online.

2. Instruct everyone to fold the sticky note into four and place it in the bag. Shake the bag so that the papers get mixed up.

3. Pass the bag back around the circle. As each child takes the bag, they should shake it again and then put their hand inside to select a paper to take out and read aloud.

4. Once read, take the sticky note and stick it on the whiteboard, clustering similar topics together to form a cyberbullying montage. Once all the ideas have been shared, review the display that's been created to explore different types of online bullying identified.

5. Conclude that while there are lots of benefits to digital technology, there is a darker side where it can be misused to threaten, harass, humiliate or embarrass. Collectively, this type of behaviour is usually referred to as online or cyberbullying.

Activity 1 (20 minutes)

1. Allocate three points in the room: 1 = True; 2 = False; 3 = Unsure.

2. Explain that you are going to read out the Activity 1: Opinion Statements and after each one you will ask the children to move to the point in the room that best reflects their opinion.

3. Encourage discussion, especially about statement 6, exploring the difference between making one thoughtless comment and sustained, targeted comments.

Activity 2 (20 minutes)

1. Suggest that people sometimes use the excuse that 'it was just banter' if they are challenged about a comment or joke made at someone else's expense. Ask if anyone has experience of this and invite the children to share any examples (within confidentiality boundaries).

2. Ask the children to work in small groups, each group with a large sheet of paper and pens to make notes. Invite a volunteer for each group to turn the paper landscape, then write the title: 'The difference between banter and bullying' across the middle, close to the top. Underneath this instruct the volunteer to draw a dividing line down the middle of the paper, writing 'Banter' as a heading on one side and 'Bullying' on the other. The task for each group is to discuss and record where they think the differences lie.

3. Allow 10–15 minutes for discussion and then invite feedback from each group. Reinforce these messages:

   ▣ A joke is only a joke if everyone laughs and nobody feels hurt, uncomfortable, disrespected or offended.

   ▣ Banter (if used at all) probably works best in real-life conversations where the impact of it can be gauged and the meaning is clear. If anyone is upset, it should always be stopped immediately and apologies made, if appropriate.

   ▣ What one person thinks is banter can be perceived as aggressive, rude, belittling or bullying behaviour by someone else.

   ▣ Any form of bullying is never acceptable.

   ▣ It is best to treat people online with the same care and consideration you would like people to treat you with in the real world.

   ▣ There are laws to protect everyone from digital bullying, particularly if the message contains aggressive, threatening or sexual content.

4. Offer this online Cambridge dictionary definition to clarify:

   ▣ *Banter*, defined as 'conversation that is funny and not serious'.[6]

   ▣ *Bullying*, defined as 'the behaviour of a person who hurts or frightens someone smaller or less powerful, often forcing that person to do something they do not want to do'.[7]

Activity 3 (20 minutes)

1. Introduce the role of 'bystanders', to mean those who might not directly join in with cyberbullying or banter but do nothing to prevent it.

2. Back in their groups, ask the children to read the scenarios on the Activity 3: The Role of a Bystander Worksheet and have a group discussion to consider:

   ▣ the role that bystanders play

   ▣ what bystanders could do to become 'upstanders' and to show support and challenge what is happening.

3. Explain that bullying is usually about power and control, and a bully has no power without 'enforcers' who join in. Liking, sharing and re-posting offensive material can normalize bullying behaviour, leading children to believe that it is acceptable to be rude, unkind or mean. Bystanders who do nothing

---

6   https://dictionary.cambridge.org/dictionary/english/banter
7   https://dictionary.cambridge.org/dictionary/english/bullying

also enable a cyberbully to gain more power and, arguably, by ignoring what is happening, condone it. If you know someone is being targeted, or you see it happening online, stand up to online bullies by challenging them, showing support for the victim, and/or reporting it. Make it clear that no one should ever put themselves at risk of harm, but bystanders can become 'upstanders' without physical contact by:

- not joining in or 'liking' nasty comments

- not sharing or re-posting

- offering support to the target

- reporting inappropriate comments to the online platform

- encouraging the victim to get help or report what is happening.

Review (15 minutes)

1. Ask each child to suggest a reason why someone may not report they are being bullied in a digital space. This could include:

   - fear that a parent will take away the device or tell them to come off a social media platform

   - not knowing who to tell

   - hoping it will stop if they ignore it

   - fear that the bullying will escalate

   - anxiety they will not be taken seriously.

2. Conclude that it can be hard to tell someone, especially if the bullying is in response to something you are embarrassed or ashamed of, but it is important to get support and report what is happening. Point out that internet providers and social media networks want to clamp down on bullies, not least because most of their revenue comes from advertising and big companies will not want to be associated with it and they could lose money.

3. Give out details of local support services and signpost to in-school support available.

4. For support with bullying call the National Bullying Helpline[8] or contact Childline.[9]

---

8   www.nationalbullyinghelpline.co.uk/contact.html
9   www.childline.org.uk

ACTIVITY 1: OPINION STATEMENTS

1. I have the right to say whatever I like on social media.

   False: While everyone has the right to post online, content that targets those with a characteristic protected by the Equality Act 2010 (including gender, ethnicity, faith and sexual orientation) may constitute hate speech or a hate crime, which is an offence in the UK. Most online providers and social media platforms also have rules for posting content, which should be adhered to. Those that don't may be blocked, reported or suspended or their account closed.

2. If someone doesn't like what I post, that's their problem.

   False: We all have a responsibility to think about what we post and how it might be received by others. While we won't always agree or like what people share, we should be respectful of different opinions.

3. If someone posts a bad 'selfie' they should expect people to laugh at them.

   False: Laughing, mocking or making cruel comments about someone's physical appearance is never acceptable. While one nasty comment would not usually be considered cyberbullying, if it continues or targets a protected characteristic, it may be part of wider illegal behaviour, such as hate crime.

4. Someone can only cyberbully you if you let them.

   False: Cyberbullying is not something you can consent to.

5. Only girls engage in online bullying.

   False: Cyberbullying is not gender-specific behaviour.

6. Having an online argument is not the same as bullying.

   True: A one-off online argument in itself is unlikely to be considered cyberbullying, which is defined as deliberate and repeated behaviour.

7. It is everyone's responsibility to report online bullying.

   True: As digital citizens, we all have a collective responsibility to report online harm, including bullying. Social media platforms have easy report mechanisms or you can tell a trusted adult to get help and support.

8. Making harsher punishments for people caught bullying online would result in fewer people doing it.

   Unsure: Some people believe this while others think that because the online community is so large it would be impossible to enforce harsh punishments. This topic could be developed into a wider discussion to explore children's values and attitudes.

ACTIVITY 3: THE ROLE OF A BYSTANDER

Case study 1
Sam shares a joke he thinks is hilarious with his friends on social media. The joke makes fun of women drivers, so he adds the hashtags #whywomenshouldntdrive and #carsareformen. Of the 100 people who see it, 57 think it's funny too so they re-post and share it with their followers, using the same hashtags; 19 just 'like' it; 11 scroll past without looking; and 13 people are deeply offended so report him to the social media network.

Case study 2
Raj is angry when Tommy beats him in a spelling test. Raj usually comes top and feels humiliated when the rest of the class tease him for coming second. To get his own back he creates a poll called 'We Hate Tommy' asking everyone in the class to vote to remove Tommy from their messaging group. He also posts a meme of someone cheating in a test with #WhyIhateTommy embedded in it. The meme is quickly liked and shared widely by other children in the class, who add other reasons to hate Tommy in the comment box.

Case study 3
Jude has been best friends with Zara since they were little but now Zara has a boyfriend, Abe, she seems to have no time for Jude. Jude feels jealous and angry; she wants her friend back. Determined to split them up she sets up a fake profile on social media to pose as Abe's ex-girlfriend and sends friendship requests to Zara and everyone they know. Her plan is working, everyone has accepted her request so now all she has to do is make up loads of bad things about Abe so that Zara breaks up with him.

Case study 4
Roman has been receiving threats via text and social media. He thinks he knows who is doing it but can't be sure as the username keeps changing. He has blocked the texts, but he loves social media and doesn't see why he should be forced to close his account. He is starting to feel paranoid and can't help himself looking around at school and trying to work out who is responsible. He always thought he had lots of friends but now feels very alone. Everyone must see what is happening, so why haven't they said anything?

LESSON 5: KEEPING SAFE IN THE DIGITAL WORLD

Aim

This lesson contains activities to consider the sort of information willingly given out online and in social media compared to that disclosed in the real world to strangers, and to explore the potential risks, as well as benefits, of making new friends online. This includes learning to recognize situations where they feel nervous, worried or scared and how to respond if someone asks them to do something they do not want to.

Learning outcomes

- Understand the risks of posting personal information online, especially that which can be used to identify you.

- Recognize that people online are not always who they say they are.

- Understand that grooming and child sexual exploitation are not new things and digital technology does not cause or allow them, but it can enable them.

- Understand the importance of staying safe online and reporting concerns.

Note: Some activities in this lesson may not be age-appropriate for younger children so please check to assess and adapt if required.

Time: 140 minutes

Resources

- Activity 2: Online Safety Statements

- Whiteboard and pens

- Copies of Activity 4: Rose and Charlotte (cut up into episodes)

- The Child Exploitation and Online Protection Centre (CEOP) website: www.ceop.police.uk/Safety-Centre (research before the lesson to find details of how to report online concerns)

- Paper and pens

- Copies of Lesson 6: Review Quiz

How to do it
Introduction (15 minutes)

1. Start by offering this quote to provoke comments and discussion about what it means and to test the validity of it.

   'A friend may be waiting behind a stranger's face.' (Maya Angelou)[10]

2. Ask:

   - Where are you likely to meet new friends in the real world?

     Answers could include the following:

     - Someone new starting at school

     - Being introduced by a friend

     - At a club (e.g. sports, faith group, uniformed organization or youth club)

     - On holiday

     - Through family

     - Starting secondary school.

   - What information are you likely to share from the start?

     Suggest that it takes time to build a new friendship but things you may tell someone on first meeting could include the following:

     - Your first name

     - The area, not the address, you live in

     - Your year at school, but not the school

     - Things you like/dislike

     - Hobbies.

     Point out that these things give a bit of information about who you are but not the private details of where you can be found, which you might tell someone once you know them better and have built trust.

   - What would stop you telling someone new personal and private things about yourself?

     Answers could include the following:

---

10 https://quotecatalog.com/quote/maya-angelou-a-friend-may-be-R1kG451 (taken from *Letter to My Daughter*, 2009)

- Not trusting them yet

- Feeling that it is inappropriate

- Intuition

- Not feeling safe

- Not knowing them well enough to confide.

Activity 1 (15 minutes)

1. With the children working in groups, ask them to discuss the benefits and drawbacks to making new friends online. Ideas can be recorded under the headings 'Benefits' and 'Drawbacks'. Examples include:

   Benefits: easier to talk online; meet people regardless of where you live; find people with shared interests; give and receive support; practice communication skills; learn from each other, make new friends or even find love.

   Drawbacks: people do not always tell the truth; can't see body language or hear tone of voice, you may be asked to do something you are uncomfortable with; talking to someone much older or inappropriate in some other way; you can be targeted for grooming.

2. Invite each group in turn to share their key points, reinforcing that many children and young people enjoy communities online, where peers come together to share a common interest. There are also many who have found comfort from online support groups. Conclude that it is a good idea to be as cautious online as you would be in the real world to reduce the risks of anyone misleading, cheating, lying or trying to make inappropriate contact.

Activity 2 (40 minutes)

1. Invite the children to listen as you read the Activity 2: Online Safety Statements. Select the most age-appropriate statements for the children participating, adapting any that aren't suitable or leaving them out. After each one, the children should move to the designated point in the room that best reflects their opinion:

   - Point A: This is safe.

   - Point B: This is potentially unsafe.

2. Take time to discuss responses after each statement, including how appropriate or inappropriate the request is and why. After this, children can move places on the opinion spectrum if they want to.

3. Suggest that talking to parents/carers openly about the social media platforms you use can reduce anxiety and reassure them that you are putting safety first. Make it clear that it is inappropriate for unknown adults to be approaching children online, 'liking' content, asking questions or sending suggestive emojis. Explain the importance of telling someone and reporting it to the social media provider if an adult makes you feel anxious, uncomfortable or frightened, so that steps can be taken to keep everyone safe.

Activity 3 (15 minutes)

1. Introduce the Child Exploitation and Online Protection Centre (CEOP) website.[11] CEOP is part of the National Crime Agency and the website can be used to report any online communication that has made a child feel worried, anxious or scared. This includes online bullying as well as other forms of online abuse, including grooming for exploitation.

2. With the children in pairs, invite them to familiarize themselves with the website, selecting three key pieces of information to share back in the wider group.

Activity 4 (45 minutes)

1. Divide the children into small working groups, giving each group paper and pens to make notes on. Explain that this is a storytelling activity, which will be told in episodes. Rose and Charlotte are not real people, but the story is based on real events. After each episode, the children will discuss the questions posed and agree some key points to share back in the wider group when the story ends.

2. Give out episodes 1–3 from Activity 4: Rose and Charlotte, one at a time, allowing up to ten minutes for the children to read and respond to the contents. Alternatively, facilitate by reading the episodes aloud and then giving out the questions for the children to work on in groups.

3. Hold back the final instalment, which is below. Bring everyone back together, read the story so far, stopping to invite key points from the different group discussions, including different perceptions of the online friendship, the role of the parent and the way that photo sharing is introduced.

4. Finally, read aloud the ending where 'Charlotte' is revealed to be an online predator:

---

11 www.ceop.police.uk/Safety-Centre

FINAL EPISODE

Rose is heartbroken. She has sent loads of messages to Charlotte, but she hasn't received one back for days. She can't work out what has gone wrong. She thought they were best friends; she has done everything that Charlotte asked of her, even though she wasn't 100 per cent comfortable with sending the bath pics. It wasn't her fault that Charlotte ran out of credit so couldn't send her own. In fact, she realizes, she doesn't have any photos of Charlotte, apart from her profile pic on the gaming site where they met. She wishes she did, at least then she'd have something to remind her while she waits for her friend to respond.

Meanwhile, Charlotte, who is actually a 37-year-old man called Paul, has been arrested by the police. On his computer they find hundreds of pyjama and bathtime pics sent by girls aged between 10 and 13. There are other inappropriate images and explicit messages that he has screenshot, saved and widely shared with adults who have a similar unhealthy interest in children.

The police consider him a high risk to children and pledge to do their best to get justice for his victims. A local police officer gets ready to visit Rose and her parents to break the news.

5. Explain that this story describes a child being groomed. Define grooming as a deliberate action by an adult to build an emotional relationship with a child for the purpose of inappropriate sexual contact and/or a relationship. This can include the taking and/or distribution of inappropriate images and enticing a child to create them. For younger children, you may want to shorten this definition to an adult who wants to befriend children with the purpose of abusing them. Children can be groomed online or face to face, by a stranger or someone they know – for example, a family member, friend or adult in a position of trust.

6. Ask the children if they noticed any clues that 'Charlotte' might not have been who she said she was and could present a threat. Answers could include:

   ▪ How quickly the friendship developed.

   ▪ How Charlotte encouraged Rose to drop her other friends and rely on her.

   ▪ Charlotte's keenness to use an encrypted messaging service so that Rose's mother couldn't see their messages.

   ▪ How quickly Charlotte came up with the plan to change her username to continue the deception.

   ▪ That Charlotte only had a profile photo.

   ▪ That Rose and Charlotte had no shared 'friends' or 'followers'.

THE POSITIVE RELATIONSHIPS CLASSROOM ACTIVITY BOOK

- That all of Charlotte's dares included the removal of clothes.

- That only Rose completed the dares – Charlotte always had an excuse.

7. Explain that while it can be hard to tell if a profile is fake, there are a few indicators to look out for. These include being wary of profiles that do not have many photos, friends or details about the person. Look out for inconsistencies in the information given, such as age, location or interests. Do a search for other social media accounts, and if these don't match up, it's probably because they're not being truthful. The message here is not to send any information, and break off contact if you feel even slightly unsure or distrustful. There is no obligation to keep speaking to anyone online, whoever they say they are.

8. Suggest that it is far safer to only accept friendship requests from people known in the real world and to block requests from anyone who isn't. Sometimes a groomer will assume a different persona, for example pretend to be a child (as in the story), but other styles of grooming include those who do not hide their identity but attract children in other ways, maybe by listening, being kind and sympathetic, or offering incentives like gifts, money or a chance to become famous. In some cases, parents/carers are groomed too in order to build trust and gain access.

9. Point out that grooming can take place over months, often without a child realizing that it is happening.

10. Also warn against complying with requests to move off a social media platform to direct messaging apps like WhatsApp, which are end-to-end-encrypted, meaning that no one can see what is sent and received. This method of grooming is commonly used by organized crime gangs, including County Lines, to exploit children for sexual and criminal purposes.

Although direct messaging is a perfectly safe form of communication when used responsibly, best advice for children is to show a trusted adult if they receive a DM request. Any concerning messages can then be screenshot (for evidence) and the sender blocked and reported.

11. Give a summary that makes it clear that grooming children for abuse and/or exploitation is illegal. Reassure the children that their safety is protected by law. They will be taken seriously if they report anyone that has approached them, sent inappropriate content, tricked them or done anything else that makes them feel uncomfortable, scared or anxious. Encourage them to always tell a parent/carer (or another trusted adult) in the first instance, who can support and advise them what to do next. This should include notifying the online platform and the police. Make it clear that every complaint is taken seriously and that they will not be in

trouble, even if they have broken online rules (e.g. ignoring age regulations). A victim is never to blame for their abuse.

Review (15 minutes)

1. Use the simple Lesson 6: Review Quiz to check understanding and reinforce learning, either by completing it individually or asking the whole class the questions and choosing different children to give the answers.

2. Quiz answers (1 point for every correct answer)

   1: a, c and d
   2: a, b and d
   3: b
   4: d, e and f
   5: d, e and f
   6: c, d, e and f

3. Ask the children to swap quizzes, so they don't mark their own, and go through the quiz. The pair with the most correct answers should be congratulated for their online safety knowledge.

4. Conclude that while this lesson focused on the misuse of digital technology, including grooming via social media and gaming platforms, there has always been a small minority of adults who pose a threat to children. Digital technology is not at fault, it just facilitates the user. Remembering the ways to stay safe and using them every time you use digital technology will help keep everyone safe and make cyberspace a nicer place to be, so that we can all enjoy it.

Extension activity

For older children, consider setting them the task of finding out more about the Online Safety Act 2023[12] and the protection it aims to provide users of digital technology, especially children under the age of 18. This information can be presented to the rest of the class, or a younger year group, at a later date.

---

12 www.legislation.gov.uk/ukpga/2023/50/enacted

ACTIVITY 2: ONLINE SAFETY STATEMENTS

1. One of your followers asks you to like their new profile photo.

2. Someone whose username you don't recognize claims you both go to the same school.

3. You get left angry messages after posting comments about a music video you didn't like.

4. An unknown adult likes your photo and sends an emoji wink.

5. You get sent a link to an online competition. Complete it to win a year's free subscription to a well-known streaming site.

6. A friend is pressuring you to set up a profile on a social media platform you are not old enough to join.

7. Your mum posts a baby photo of you on her social media.

8. An online gaming friend asks lots of questions about how happy you are at home.

9. You download a track from a music streaming platform, not realizing it has explicit content.

10. Someone claiming to be a model scout invites you to an online meeting platform so they can see you better.

11. Your sports team posts a team picture to celebrate a win without asking permission.

12. You are asked to like and share a meme that makes fun of a particular group of people.

13. A friend of a friend asks where you live in a group chat.

ACTIVITY 4: ROSE AND CHARLOTTE

Episode 1

Rose is best friends with Charlotte. They are both 12 years old and spend hours talking, laughing and having fun together via multiple apps and social media platforms. Rose knows what Charlotte likes and doesn't like, why she argues with her little brother and the colour paint she chose for her bedroom last year. Charlotte knows what Rose's favourite dinner is, her shoe size and why she doesn't get on with the other girls in her class. As Charlotte often says, they don't need anyone else, they have each other.

However, Rose and Charlotte have never met in real life. They don't even live in the same city. They met on a gaming site, played together, then started direct messaging and their friendship blossomed from there.

When Rose's mum discovers this, she is shocked. She knew Rose spoke to Charlotte every day, but assumed they were school friends. She tells her daughter that in her day she was only friends with people she could go and visit.

1. Why do you think Rose's mum is shocked?

2. Is it possible to be friends with someone you don't know in real life?

3. How do online friendships compare to those in the real world?

Episode 2

Rose tries to explain to her mum that everyone has friends online nowadays. She tells her mum how much Charlotte means to her, how much they have in common, that she has never had such a close friend before. Her mother is not convinced. She tells Rose to get off her phone and make friends with the girls in her class. She threatens to take the phone away if she doesn't.

As soon as her mum leaves the room, Rose texts Charlotte. Within seconds Charlotte suggests they communicate via an end-to-end encrypted messaging app from now on. She says she will change her username to Josie, a girl in Rose's class so her mum can't check what they are doing, and no one can see their messages. To make her point, Rose gets a message notification from 'Josie' and when she opens it, Charlotte has sent a picture of a witch labelled 'Rose's mum'. Rose laughs, her mum will never know what she is doing now!

1. How might the threat Rose's mum made affect what happens now?

2. Why do you think Charlotte suggests keeping their friendship hidden? Why does Rose agree so quickly?

3. Are there any risks to carrying out the plan to only use encrypted services and change names?

Episode 3

The plan is working. Rose tells her mum she and Josie are now friends and her mum replies that she is happy her daughter has stopped wasting time talking online. Meanwhile, Rose and Charlotte continue to do just that for hours, often until well after midnight. Tonight, while messing about, Charlotte dares Rose to send photos of her in her pyjamas. Rose sends one immediately and then some more of her in bed with her teddy bear waving goodnight. They are both disappointed when Charlotte's parents unexpectedly come into her room, so she can't send a pyjama pic back. To make up for it, Charlotte promises to go one better and send a photo of her in the bath tomorrow.

Rose can't stop laughing. Charlotte is so daring but she's glad her mum won't find out; she doesn't have a sense of humour when it comes to pranks like this.

1. What do you think motivated Charlotte to challenge Rose to send pyjama pics?

2. Why do you think Rose accepted Charlotte's dare so quickly?

3. Is Rose's mum right not to like 'pranks' like this? Why/why not?

4. Can you identify any other potential risks in this friendship?

LESSON 6: REVIEW QUIZ

Read each question and tick all of the correct answers.

1. Ways to stay safe when using digital technology include:

    a. Only accepting friendship requests from people you know and trust.

    b. Only using it after 6pm.

    c. Using privacy settings.

    d. Never giving out your address or contact details.

2. Potential indicators of a fake profile are:

    a. Few photos.

    b. A small number of friends or followers.

    c. A big red danger sign.

    d. Inconsistent information about the person.

3. CEOP stands for:

    a. Children Expect and Order Protection Centre.

    b. Child Exploitation and Online Protection Centre.

    c. Child Expedition and Outdoor Pursuits Centre.

    d. Chickens Elephants and Ostriches Park Centre.

4. If you are sent an inappropriate picture or message, you should:

    a. Send a rude message back.

    b. Ask the person not to do it.

    c. Forward it to friends.

    d. Report it to the digital provider.

    e. Tell a trusted adult.

    f. Consider reporting it to the police and CEOP.

5. If you are asked to take and send inappropriate content or do anything that makes you feel uncomfortable you should:

   a. Tell the person to go away.

   b. Keep talking until they persuade you it is safe.

   c. Ignore and delete.

   d. Report it to the digital provider.

   e. Tell a trusted adult.

   f. Report it to the police and CEOP.

6. Everyone can stay safer online and when using social media if they:

   a. Never use it.

   b. Only use it under adult supervision.

   c. THINK before they post (is it True, is it Helpful, is it Inspiring? Is it Necessary? Is it Kind?).

   d. Use the security settings provided.

   e. Don't like or share unkind or harmful content – be a digital upstander.

   f. Block and report anything that makes them feel concerned, anxious, worried or scared.